STREET CHRISTIAN DEVIL

A SINGULAR POETIC PERSPECTIVE

Trenton Scott

WALDENHOUSE PUBLISHERS, INC.
WALDEN, TENNESSEE

STREET CHRISTIAN DEVIL:
a singular poetic perspective

Cover Art by Jeremy Adams
Published by Waldenhouse Publishers, Inc.
100 Clegg Street, Signal Mountain, Tennessee 37377 USA
888-222-8228   www.waldenhouse.com
Printed in the United States of America
Type and Design by Karen Paul Stone
ISBN: 978-1-947589-38-4 perfect bound (paperback)
ISBN: 978-1-947589-39-1 case bound (hardback)
Library of Congress Control Number: 2021930403
134 poems abstractly illustrating the trials and tribulations of life within the Schizoaffective mind of the author's alter ego, Street Christian Devil. - provided by Publisher
POETRY / Subjects & Themes / General
POETRY / Subjects & Themes / Inspirational & Religious
POETRY / Subjects & Themes / Death, Grief, Loss

To

My mother, Shannon Cline

4

Contents

8

FOREWORD

The mind of a person is an amazing place; sometimes it is busy and sometimes it can be more like ping pong balls bouncing back and forth in an empty room. The mind of a person can compute, send messages to aid in our survival, and in general help us to experience the world as humans. It can be a confusing and terrifying place, too, for those of us who have been exposed to trauma, or who suffer from chemical imbalances in the brain which affect day-to-day living, or both. My brother's mind on its own is remarkable. He was in the top of his class in air traffic control school and he is one of the smartest people I know, but he is more than a mind. He is also a heart and a soul. He was a good Sailor and he is a good man. I am biased, but I don't hesitate to say that I love him very much even though he can annoy the stew out of me in a way only siblings can.

I am so excited for you to get to read his poetry and, in a way, catch a glimpse of his unique perspective on life, living, love, and loss. He writes with a vulnerability and honesty uncharacteristic of many who have had an experience similar to his. Where some might seek to hide their struggles and pieces of themselves which are not easy for others to digest, my brother has chosen to share even the broken pieces. He has chosen to arrange them in this book alongside his fonder musings like a beautiful, chaotic stained-glass window. I encourage you to enjoy this work of art for what it is: a collection of experiences skillfully expressed with honesty and courage.

Trace Cline

PREFACE

In 1998, I wrote my first poem entitled, *Tomorrow.* Years passed by and my poetry became dormant. In 2010, what started out as a happenstance writing session, morphed into much more than therapy; poetry became a passion in which I could express myself in a way that was unique to the personality that my genetics and environment created, both at birth and from experiencing life. I didn't have a computer or a typewriter to record and file this passion. However, I did have a smart phone. I began to write. One poem became many.

Years passed by and it became clear that at least one purpose in my life was to tell stories and convey thoughts through rhyme. I began developing a following on social media. A book in the Library of Congress along with a songwriting career became goals. In order to make these goals a reality, I decided that my years of work, all filed away on a smart phone, needed to be introduced to the public. *Street Christian Devil* was born. Over the next ten chapters, I hope to touch on every emotion as I explain who I am, unconventionally. In the end, you will be the judge as to whether or not that goal was attained.

ACKnOWLEDGMEnts

My appreciation for the cover art goes to Jeremy Adams.

This book wouldn't have been possible without certain people that, at some point, had a heavy influence on my life. Special love and thanks to the following people:

Carden and Hazel Ford, W. A. McNeece, Lois Manley, Wayne and Shirley McNeece, Arvil and Flossie Scott, Christine Cline, Jerry and Karen Cline, Doyle and Patricia Roy, Anna "Mama Ann" Jones, Billy and Wanda Isom, Donnie and Sheila Davidson, Jan Scott, Anthony Webb Scott, Terry and Shawn Brewer, Mark and Darla Blazek, Mike and Von Cline, Scott and Lynne Cline, Shawn Tawater, Jon and Kristin Jones, Greg Roy, Greg Bolton, Rodney Bolton, Matthew Davidson, Jonathon Davidson, Michael Davidson, Eric Scott, Justin Holloway, Erin Holloway, Haley Brewer, Trevor and Casey Brewer, Tyler and Blair Brewer, Brett and Chelsea Woodard, Shane McNeece, Stuart Cain, Bill Womack, Tim Templeton, Debbie Turner, Elijah and Elizabeth Grimm, Brandon and Emily White, Ben Cline, Delaney Cline, Annalee Cline, Zackary Scott, Lexi and Mia Scott, Damon and Amber Dees, Dalton and Carson Dees, Taylor and Amy Cline, Denver Haynes and Carden Cline, Trace and Elizabeth Cline, Jane Elizabeth Cline, Eddie and Lynn Bassham, Brandon and Keyta Bassham, Larry and Peggy McNeece, Margaret Norman, Wade McNeece, Bradly McNeece, Paul and Diana Kersey, Nathan Kersey, William Davis, Kevin Nelson, Howard Bartholomew Barnwell III, Tony and Janie Brawner,

Amy Brawner, Ray Brawner, Christopher Blazek, Nicklaus Blazek, Jonathon Blazek, Courtney Butler, Jamie Hughes, Gary and Jennifer Bradford, Brian and Candi Nelson, Jacklyn Mullins, Christopher and Staci Robinson, Jennifer Boehm, Keri Smith, Treva Ritts, Dr. Christy Price, Jeanne Brady, Bradley and Kristy Pennington, Rob Forgey, Jackie Neal, Alisha Campbell, Deaneen Cochran, Myra Cochran, James and Tara Lyles, Arthur and Debbie Boehm, Bobby Ledford, Matthew Ledford, Nathan Ledford, Barry and Dawn Wymbs, Rebekah Reyher, Tim and Katie Walker, Jerry "Boog" Evans, Becky Pennington, Shanella Stacey, Windell Robbins, Todd and Misty Queen, Sam and Vickie Brown, Stacey Travis, Craig and Jaime Overturf, Claude Croft, Rosalind Richee, Jennifer Hoops, Christopher Blackwood, Jerry and Jennifer Leonard, Chudi "Albert" Mathenge Ndegwa, and last, but certainly not least, my mother and father, J. Douglas and Shannon Cline.

Chapter One

Please allow me a moment to introduce myself the only way that I know how. Growing up, all I wanted to be was a professional baseball player. I have delusions, a symptom of Schizoaffective Disorder, that I indeed made it to the big leagues, and I love to drift off into the great beyond pondering the memories that seem so very real to me. However, life had other plans.

Tutorial

Being alone means getting stoned
Constant search for the perfect rhyme
Music and books broaden the horizons
Headbanging line by line showtime
Outlaw preference suitability
Cry inside death and wear a smile
Walk barefoot on glass and hot coals
Know thyself and steer clear of denial
Coast to coast dirt road traveling
No destination to go in particular
Line up your sights to pull the trigger
Homicidal words beyond vehicular
Songs take you back through time
Followed by the faintest of smells
Empty memories will bring the pain
Unknown meanings only time tells
Professor lecture in the common
Scientists were taught their profession
Pull up a chair and have a seat, doc
This is natural and class is in session

YOUR WORDS

Write us a poem
You are a poetry writer
Thank you for the words
Help me become a fighter
We feel the need for some poetry
Your words are a blessing at times
It brightens my day, it saddens me
Please help me with your rhymes
You take me back to the past
I'm the fish, your words the lure
I become hooked when I take the bait
To the words so simple and pure
Fear, hate and discrimination
Are not neglected in your artistry
You speak of racist bigots
You keep me from thinking elementary
Your words are chosen carefully
Your desire to fight the world
Not afraid to face the government
To the winds your words are unfurled
Your ability to delve deeper into my mind
Without knowing my inner thoughts
It is compassion, it is intuition
Your simplicity cannot be taught
We send you a discussion or topic
Your words do not beat around the bush
We need to keep the topics coming
And keep providing your OG Kush
Ask the poetry man to write
He will call upon a higher power
He will provide you the comfort you seek

He will help in less than an hour
This is your therapy session
There are acts that cannot persist
But he is here for your convenience
To show you that love still exists
Because you are speaking your mind
You will eventually be worldwide heard
You have me wrapped in love and hate
When you supply us with your words

BaSEBaLL

My first experience of love and passion
Derived from the first toss in the air
Consuming my every waking hour
Chasing perfection knowing I won't get there
I was three years old when I discovered
An American pastime called baseball
Love and passion exist at that age
It is innocent, complete and without flaw
It is the smell of the grass and the dirt
It is the smell of that new leather glove
It is the feel of the laces in red
It is beyond a gift from above
It's where three out of ten equals greatness
It's where four out of ten is that of legend
The possibility to stay child-like longer
It's "I have a dream" to quote the Reverend
There are no-hitters, ribbies and dingers
Grand slams, walks and suicide squeeze
Sportsmanship is learned and mastered
Accepting failure will eventually ease
Many hours are spent practicing all summer
Many games are played every Spring
How good can one get all depends
On how much time they're willing to bring
You never let me down and always encouraged
My first word was "ball" and Mom knew
That all I needed was a bat, ball and glove
And my first love would always be true

Cicada Making Noise

I write down when I've fell
Inward journeys to the depths of hell
I write down what I've done
I've lost. I've tied. I've won.
I write down what I've seen
Beyond playing ball in Dizzy Dean
I write down others suggestions
Dive deep to answer all of their questions
I write down how I feel
Knowing all the while words can kill
I write down my heartaches
Others learn from confessional mistakes
I write down how I pray
Each and every single day
I write down how I love
Satan cries to send a few back above

Ten Minutes

Break apart monotonous stability
Change direction with a complete one-eighty
Think only of yourself without company
Break the nose of Marsha Brady
Step on toes to gain unbiased attention
Write down each thought as they come
Naturally possessed inner demons
Will make a little sense to some
Eight lines have taken three minutes
Line nine is a factual statement
Line ten follows chronologically
Twelfth line shows elevens enslavement
Five minutes in and we're halfway there
Fourteen is a number I've worn
Fifteen has seen my front and back
Sixteen for Peyton Manning to adorn
Jaded by a preposterous amount
One eight for Manning in the pros
Equine tales from a manuscript
Opposition to those that oppose
The goal remains twenty-four lines
Thought to thought of my lost and found
Rhyme at the end of every other
Ten minutes of thoughts spinning 'round

Tried True and Grateful

Making too many poor decisions
I decided to sign the dotted line
Then the cab pulled up with her
Never worked by grand design
Tried true and grateful
Caves in the Arabic mountains
I will never tell a soul the story
I didn't do it for public recognition
I did it for my country's glory
Tried true and grateful
Someone has always been there
To whom I place the call all depends
Blessed to have so many options
Blessed to call so many my friends
Tried true and grateful
I held my Mamaw's hand tightly
I knew the end was on the way
I called the family to the bedside
She then heard what we had to say
Tried true and grateful
Waiting for love to start knocking
Decades of waiting by the door
Too different to be loved by another
Loneliness knocks asking for more
Tried true and grateful

Chapter Two

I cannot explain what was the driving force behind my actions, but for no particular reason, I asked for a word or subject matter on social media that I could write about. I made the promise to have a result, for those who made suggestions, in less than thirty minutes. The response to such a request was adequate enough to provide me with plenty of material. I began testing my skills. Some of the results can be found in the following chapter.

SILHOUETTE Manner

Blinding sequence of rhetorical ash
Rain drenched clouds off in the distance
Sunlight exposure direct in the eye
Solar panels yield to constant persistence
Wipers clear nature's holy water
Bring forth beauty reserved for the west
Double rainbows appear only in sunlight
Silhouette sunset with a ten second test
Darker hours catering to mystery
Unknown motives squandering Gallow
Posted further away from the street light
Capture beauty in the silhouette shadow
Street artists carry cardboard cutouts
Paint-stained fingers perfected design
Twenty minutes for the final product
Esteemed transfer to a silhouette skyline
We finally arrive at a damaged cornea
Silhouetted objects of whom you just met
Possibilities include the never ending
Gazing eyes at a permanent silhouette

WILLOW

Inspire the wind induced melody
Listen closely to canopy legend
Trained sensory fine-tuned chorus
Outside service enjoyed by the Reverend
A Willow cries flowing teardrops
Ever hanging without touching ground
Singing songs of the whispered silence
Giving shade twenty-five feet around
Give your best shot Mother Nature
Memories soaked up root deep
Let slip the secrets trespassing
Locked-in fight song taking each leap
Shielded bonfire on football Saturday
Picnic sheltered savory teaching
Longing for heartfelt embrace
Blue skies and stars forever reaching
Hollow wounds prove detrimental
Interference with the ebb and flow
New construction saves what remains
Continued legacy of the Weeping Willow

Nature's Nurture

Vice mirrored equal same synonym
Environmental mind left exposed
Monkey will see and monkey will do
Learned behavior behind doors closed
Actions force inevitable reaction
Same conclusions until actions change
Some lessons are as easy as I'm sorry
Others Curry you up from midrange
Outward guidance leads the sanity circle
Generational knowledge acquired
Tutorial from all five senses
Complete awareness is all that's required
Love is not given a character
Touch a hot fence one more time
Knee jerk reactions toss the spilled coffee
Big old Pete cannot stop on a dime
Master perfectly conceptual theory
Fail seldom and try not to boast
Rock at last on the front porch waving
Nature's nurture will teach you the most

FOR A LIVING

Fill up the school soda machines
Watch the kids as a camp counselor
Join the Navy as an air traffic controller
Work the door taking money as a bouncer
Check off selling potato chips and crackers
Drive a big rig across forty-eight states
Complete any mission by the government
Sell the beer that St. Louis creates
A substitute teacher lacks recognition
Killings bugs and rodents can be a pain
Production assistant at a carpet mill
Sell the soda that started with cocaine
Deliver pizzas for four different companies
Don't forget to hobble the mare in heat
Clean out the horse and pig stalls
Pour and level out all that concrete
Learn to build a website from scratch
Write a book and pickup recycled trash
Hustle in life and in competitive sports
Add the unspoken that I've done for cash

CODEPENDENt

Cold sweat builds all about
Blanket comforts skipped today
Too hot and too cold brainwaves
Back to the porcelain you pray
Inability to accept responsibility
Allowance at forty years old
Man-cave in mama's basement
Delegation to do what you're told
Mister mom and the housewife
Raising status without a degree
Spouses bring home the bacon
Without them, where would you be?
Companies rely on the customer
Promote the right product to sell
Strike hard. Strike true. Strike often.
Emblems provide stories to tell
Sip the last sup living large
Succulent spirits are essential
You are now free to feel normal
Your name is forever confidential

TWEnty PIctURES

It's 4:30 so I better start writing
I don't know how long it will take
Let us capture every moment tonight
Easter 2020 for history's sake
We know not where we are headed
The same as it was before this year
Cotton describes an overreaction
Under preparation relates like cashmere
Enjoy tonight at the table with family
Tell some stories or play a board game
Take pictures with mom, build with dad
That picture with mom? Build a frame
Smile as if that is what's contagious
Let the imagination run wild and free
Be the unique family that each of you are
Read the story that details Calvary
Families will prepare dinner together
Eighteenth line and I hit writer's block
Write one word at a time with each line
Pen down and drop the mic like a rock

PILLOW

Yesterday brought thunder and lightning
Last night brought raindrops and nightmares
Pacing, staring, sounds that are frightening
Human traffic incriminates witches' lairs
Sleep with one eye wide open observing
Concrete slabs, silk sheets and house flies
It's tragedy and triumph all well heard
Never wake up to see your own demise
A jacket, a shirt, some cotton and feathers
It's sweet dreams on the left side tonight
Tossing and racing thoughts grip pleasures
Entrance to kingdoms holding kryptonite
Lay thee down to sleep holding comfort
Lay thee down to sleep ye emotional pain
Chased and falling from heights unknown
Leave no doubt for society not slain
African, American, Australian and Asian
French, Mandarin, Portuguese and Creole
It matters not where you call home
Not all know the simple comforts of a pillow

OVER DEW

The sun scorches the asphalt and limestone
Penetrating every crevice unguarded
Dry earth accompanies death and survival
From great cities to lands left uncharted
A forest yearns for hydration like the desert
Dust tornadoes and floating tumbleweeds
Dodging famine during dreadful drought
A mirage of a high feast and rolling seas
Off to the distance a cloud is forming
Trust or trust not that the eyes reveal gray
Seven months without rainfall and thunder
Dissatisfied, disappointed and dismayed
As the cloud drifts closer and closer
Headlights appear off in the distance
A wrist watch confirms mid-afternoon
Wiper blades run steady and consistent
The cloud now hovers above the tree-line
Thunder rattles the entire foundation
Prepare for a long day and night of rain
Warned by all television and radio stations
Settled up by the fireplace, cup in hand
Raindrops on the roof comfort the soul
The pond and the creek are now singing
Filling up what was yesterday's dry hole
Water hazards fill up on the golf course
Swimming holes are now vibrant again
Forest birds sing a happy new lullaby
The dawn of a new celebration for man
The rain is still present when awakened
The sunset arrives as you open the door
Bringing smells of honeysuckle and mint
Dear human, your introduction to petrichor

ILLUMINatE

The breaker at the ballfield is lifted
Miss Granger gives a swish and flick
The forest reveals distant headlights
Rudolph has a nose for Saint Nick
Glow sticks are used on the golf course
Titleist bounces and rolls under the moon
The pool sparkles along with the star light
Wolves and coyotes will be singing soon
Nightlife tries to avoid the thought of it
It will draw a good night to an end
The worst of the day when it leaves us
Sun tells the time for all to begin
When you choose to stay out after dark
You are choosing to test your own fate
The crime will increase by the dozens
When the moon, not the Sun, illuminate

MORNING StaRt

Coffee brewing serves as the alarm clock
The cook beats the rooster to sunrise
Attentive to all senses plus a blessing
Listen up and keep an eye on the prize
Generations of recipes passed down
Charging batteries better known by heart
Fuel for the soul and fuel for the job
First gathering of the day is a good start
Head chair leads a forgotten thank you
Plans of the day are welcomed by all
Silverware clanging against porcelain
Television and radio morning roll call
Yesterday taught forever memories
Discussions of everyday happenstance
Deception will never be tolerated
Where the adults still wear the pants
In the holler we accept any beverage
Sausage and bacon describe our jentacular
Country ham with biscuits and gravy
Morning start is the accepted vernacular

RESPECt

Dissect the endless forgotten
How many have walked our planet?
Bones and teeth disintegration
Time carved with limestone in granite
Freeze here and now for the number
Dig to the core and start counting
It will never take a genius
To see that the bodies are mounting
Press play to rewind the footage
Repeated history day after day
Broken records singing sweet music
Drive the native away from red clay
Touch the curtain of nearby neighbors
Two houses one-foot apart
Private property lacking privacy
The end right next to the start
A box to hold my bones forever
Forever ends for every box made
Wisdom says a book lasts longer
Tell stories of battle games played
Compassion leads words to parchment
Known by verses by which to reflect
I then ask to be burned into ashes
Last request to show me respect

SCREAMER ROAD

One way in and one way out
The journey to the top of the hill
Moonlit dirt roads shine differently
Pay attention to what you might feel
Take in forever running water
Pines and black and white oak
Leave your city life in the city
'Round here live simple folk
The ghost stories are abundant
Trust every word you are told
Signs read by invitation only
The Eyes guard Screamer Road
The Eyes are around every corner
Up the grapevine, tucked in a tree
Your weapon, your booze and your toke
Newsflash: The Eyes see all three
For those that make it to the top
A piece of Heaven indeed awaits
It is across the Great Divide
Open doors to the Pearly Gates
To enter you must face the witch
Many a face she has sewn
It isn't recommended you cross her
The fact that she'll wear you is known
Once she trusts, she loves unconditional
The Eyes begin to look elsewhere
Knowledge and wisdom and guidance
Everyone is equal and treated fair
Food and water are plentiful
Homegrown hospitality
Friendships that grow into family
Screamer Road possesses the key

A VIVID LIFE

I never thought I would hallucinate
Yet it occurs from time to time
I walk around each day exhausted
Sleep is more than how it's defined
Insomnia is my comic book opposite
I'm on the other end of that spectrum
I can fall asleep standing up
I don't just have dreams, I collect them
I hope the next one isn't a nightmare
With me they happen more frequent
They follow me vividly everywhere I go
I can describe them sequence by sequence
I try not to appear disinterested
Just know that it's not as it seems
I'm fighting my nightmares and fatigue
I'm still attempting to be the real me
Please understand my predicament
I think we can all agree
I fight to stay awake and not miss anything
But at times I fall to narcolepsy

Beyond Loyal

"How have you been?" can move mountains
Any gesture to acknowledge persistence
She chewed me up and spit me out
Designated inner lack of existence
I saved her from death more than once
She cast me into the fire pits of hell
An eagle revealed she's a witchy woman
Prognostication promised time will tell
Instant attraction as a mutual agreement
Will she ever give me the time of day?
Will she ever forgive my shortcomings?
Each night and each morning I pray
The adventures will never be forgotten
I will carry her everywhere that I go
She is the light at the end of my tunnel
The hardest part is knowing what I know
She makes no apology for carrying on
She destroyed my heart like a piñata
She holds my loyalty nonetheless
She forever remains my saudade

HaLLoWEEn PaRtY

Halloween is around the corner
As are many memorial gardens
The sheer number of sins contained
Beware of the bones given pardons
Once every year they begin to arise
A bell warning strikes twelve times
The daylight will never protect you
Prey to those of vicious crimes
What they seek is the heart and lungs
Feel blood flow and breathe in air
We never see them on the news
Lightning quick and unheard prayer
A purge of death and destruction
Zero witnesses to be found
Family will think that you vanished
Crawling six feet from under ground
Collagen and calcium lay waiting
One-way trip on the death ferry
Lay me down to rest in pieces
Pick any bone-filled cemetery

PHantaSMIC EUPHORIa

Take this to gain a little confidence
Take a drag and make sure to inhale
Slide an eight ball across the pool table
Pharmaceutical longing to sell
Ecstatic X finds a tongue double barreled
Tracking veins for the very last time
Intensely excited endorphins
Battery acid to leave you sublime
Every cell in the body convinced
Money waits for the body to call
Coca leaves with peyote cacti
Natural tetrahydrocannabinol
Add to the highest of ratings
Football tickets need to be ripe
Know the content and potency
Search for the perfect glass pipe
Athletic conventional victory
Serotonin and dopamine view
Exhaustion collapses the lungs
From zero to twenty-six point two
Ball and chains blanketed heavily
Creation of phantasmagoria
Angels await the overzealous
Demons call seeking euphoria

BLESSED

Six are surrounding you
In more ways than one
You are given the option
Which of you face the gun?
In your mind, it's an easy decision
Nobody dies because of you
The catch is you have to jump
150 feet above the waterfall blue
You look over the edge
This is your certain death
You see a small little crevice
In the waterfall at twelve-foot depth
If you could only land
On the rock that protrudes enough
You could maybe land and fall backwards
A billion-to-one odds would be tough
Your last words are, please don't hurt her
As you take one last look around
The gun is still pointed at you
Then you hear that clicking sound
You look up with faithful whispers
You utter one final prayer to keep
You line yourself up with the protruding rock
And you take the ultimate leap
Did you survive against all odds?
Did you fall against the waterfall walls?
You survived and wrote of the discovery
Of the walkway underneath the falls

BLaCK DEatH

Who has the power to release it?
Who is running this show?
To say that it can't happen again
Above the confines and below
You are protectors of the universe
You keep most outbreaks from occurring
But I cannot ignore the possibility
Re-occurrence is so feasible, it's disturbing
Is it coincidence in the first place?
Way back in the fourteenth century
It traveled by trade from Asia
Intentionally, by accident, it's a mystery
It is interesting to think about
Assessing the situation as a society
It wiped out sixty percent of Europe
It created Gregorian propriety
There are hidden rooms in this world
That can take down an entire culture
Are they controlled by ethical standards?
Are they controlled by satirical vultures?
We are waiting to discover the answers
We are preparing for you to invade
To have that much power is daunting
You have the death of the next Black Plague

UΠDECIDED/COMMItтED

Concede Yankees unquestionable greatness
Kentucky Wildcats are basketball champs
Hockey town lives in Detroit, Michigan
Mannings hold the best quarterback camps
Who is the greatest quarterback ever?
Montana or Manning or Brady
Rings on their fingers tell the story
Only one of those quarterbacks are shady
King James or His Airness or The Mamba
Take a seat and join the endless debate
Bird and Magic and a man named Pistol Pete
All depends on your birthplace and birthdate
Champions are crowned every season
There are those that are quick to vacillate
There are those that win by the rules
There are those that win by Deflategate
Do your homework and always talk trash
If you can't pick a team don't be braggin'
Death or victory on a southeastern Saturday
Jump not from bandwagon to bandwagon

HinDSIGHt

Assassination of MLK and Kennedy
Jim Morrison will never open the door
Heroin filling veins in the fast Layne
Hanging vet coming home from war
Rehabilitation behind stoned regrets
Priceless Love that you did not pursue
Given chance to make a difference
A trigger with an aim measured true
Instant gratification to be desired
Lying tongue sways gullible belief
Run a red light and a red stop sign
Permanent erosion of a coral reef
Elected officials set out to conquer
Malpractice insurance covers ole doc
Poverty stricken saints falsely accused
Innocent to guilty with one little rock
Conventional orgasmic fantasy abort
Breaking bad took a step past crack
Last words at an unspoken deathbed
All moments that you can't take back

Senses

Are there five senses or are there more?
We know of the ones we are taught
My attempt to help you know what I'm doing
Will bring you depth or leave you distraught
It brings back the greatest of memories
The smells, the walk and the radio
It was John and Bill in the rafters
It was packing our things and let's go
It was breakfast on Saturday morning
It was Section N, seat thirty-two
What I look at consists of me also
Young horses joined a wilder crew
It also has a precious metal inside
Valued collectibles fit for all kings
It shows the GOAT alongside number twelve
Eight MVP's and eight Super Bowl rings
I wrapped it with glass and wiped off the dust
I surrounded it by wood to keep it warm
It would be fitting to be found in a diner
A trophy room, a museum or one's dorm
Ask a question and I'll tell you the answer
I promise I know every stat
Now that I have explained what it is
Tell me, what am I looking at?

CHapteR THREE

Faith is something very important to me. Throughout my life, I have placed a lot of trust in whom I believe to be my creator. At times, I have felt unworthy of forgiveness. I have felt helplessness and pain that will be discussed later on. There are certain stories of certain people that I tend to recall when my faith is in jeopardy. I cannot speak for God and my words are simply that, one man's words of faith and guidance. It is my hope to convey a David versus Goliath take on life, whereas the faith of a mustard seed not only must be present, but also trusted. When it is time, the roller coaster of emotions will commence.

TOMORROW

Do not look back on yesterday
For it is in the past
Do not lose sight of what today has to offer
For it may be thy last
Tomorrow has a faithful definition
Perhaps a dream that we portray
Will tomorrow ever get here?
For the day is always today
For thine cannot be certain
The Sun will rise again
Take the time to close thine eyes
And ask forgiveness for thy sins
You will find that miracles really do happen
And that thou hath just been blind
Tomorrow exists in the Kingdom of Heaven
Therefore, seek and ye shall find
So do not worry, mother
Please do not shed sorrow
For if I cannot see you today
I will see you forever, tomorrow

Mama Ann

The definition of legacy
How can it be described?
It is written all around us
Just take a look inside
It reads 4 o'clock in the morning
It answers through dusk or dawn
Its dedication never wavered
First lesson: Pick up and move on
Its professions consist of medicine
There are leaders and witnesses too
There are Angels who have gone to Heaven
This family is me and you
Our matriarch is indescribable
She is the Angel that guided our youth
We are better people because of her discipline
Her tactics have proved tried and true
We love you with all that we are
You instructed us to be the best we can be
If only your walls could tell stories
The truth is we are your legacy
We lost Pop at forty-seven
God blessed us with JJ as part of the crew
Forever grateful for the love and lessons
We are the children of Second Avenue

SUNFLOWER

How do you put this into words?
How do you explain the emotions it brings?
Is why a question never answered?
Look closer. Every child sings
The courage displayed has to be witnessed
We have it documented on video
You live on through mementos and memories
With whom you now reside, we all know
I think of your strength and your wisdom
The lives you've touched cannot be measured
We hear your angelic voice on holidays
The love you taught will never be severed
I think of the strength of your father
I think of how he also lost your Mom
I hear the words "show me the way to go"
The answers are written in Psalms
You taught him to fully trust in God
I think of how long it has been
Know he continues to walk forward
He leaves no doubt he'll see you again
I want him to see the sunflower
The persona that you inspired
I know it hurts him to see it
But your faith to this day is admired
Cancer took you from him
Your faith and courage live on
We want to provide him with what you deserve
To be honored forever is where you belong
Childhood cancer is a nightmare
And until it ceases to exist
We honor each child in your memory

Because you were the best of the best
We cry, we laugh, we rejoice
You come to us every spring
You are forever The Sunflower
You're not here but we still hear you sing

Sacrifice

He is the only perfect human
He cures the blind and the deaf
He turns water into wine
He turns you right when you're going left
He helps you face your demons
He is stronger than they'll ever be
The proof exists in one's heart
The first step will help you see
He invites you to believe
He saves those that have been lost
He loves you unconditionally
That's why He died there on that cross
It takes great faith and courage
To believe in what you cannot see
Everything is explained in Matthew
Of how He died for you and me
His father sent Him to us
Mary was chosen to be mother of a King
We worship The Word on Sundays
We pay alms. We study. We sing.
The kindness in a true Christian's heart
Will show itself from time to time
We believe in helping and giving
We believe in the Great Divine
If you are ever seeking forgiveness
Just drop down to your knee
Accept Jesus as your Savior
Your new vision will be 20/20
You will be welcome in God's Kingdom
You will understand God's sacrifice
You will forever live in peace and harmony
Jesus already paid the price

MERCY

Her buttons are pressed by fallen angels
Her heart is protected by Grace
Temptations of the greatest evils
Last ditch effort for Satan to save face
His determined greed and anger repulse
Late, reads the clock on the tower
A beacon still shines right above her
Christ comforts her in the darkest hour
She trusts in His life that still lives
Known by Christ and Jesus and JC
The Father, the Son and the Holy Ghost
Unwavering love, serenity and mercy
He doubted that her heart was impenetrable
He tried reaching her time and again
He knew not that her soul is protected
Votes left uncounted gives Jesus the win

REDEMPtion

Choice to choose forever up or down
Never ending years to suffer or thrive
Tearful confessions of a true believer
Powerfully driven with a will to survive
The ultimate price laying on the table
For you and I, the cost is quite cheap
Open hearts for the willing and able
Each have a soul for prayers to keep
His Word gives direction and cleansing
His music leaves a mark deep within
His lessons give off an eternal light
A virgin Mother of a Son without sin
Blood did not drop when He poured
Other voices unspoken when He spoke
Pain in disciples when He was taken
Rejoice for all mankind when He awoke
A retrieval to recover paid reclamation
The debt you have yet to pay forward
An invoice to receive your redemption
Cashed in by you, given by the Lord

PURPOSE

What is left without right?
What is right without wrong?
What is wet without dry?
What is a choir without a song?
What is faith without direction?
What is direction without the South?
What is a swamp without reptiles?
What is a snake without a mouth?
Flip the script and turn it around
What if Kennedy and King were alive?
What if Kobe and Gia took a cab?
Would there be a crash to survive?
If Pharmaceuticals didn't exist
How many drugs could no longer kill?
If welfare was never an option
New responsibility for the monthly bill
A child without parents is an orphan
Religion without a deity is insane
Insanity is creation without a chance
Purpose is Christ absorbed our pain

Chapter Four

After an encounter with inspiration and hope brought on by one explanation of faith and perseverance, it is only natural to meet the devil within. For those of you who choose to enter, darkness lies in wait.

Estranged

I'm the entity of Abrahamic religions
I wanted the power of God
I was cast out of Heaven for Pride
My mind gave me a false facade
I was declared the ruler of fallen angels
And God the Unchangeable Changer
But I have the power of influence
To grow my power of hate and anger
I am a conniving manipulator
I pick on the weak and strong
Greed, Power and Control
From these I win right versus wrong
You will never see me coming
But I'm whispering in your ear
You will soon be joining me
I hunt prey three sixty-five a year
I tempted the rib of Adam
I tempted Job through my evil alley
I finally gave up on Job's mix of atoms
I'm planting my seeds in other valleys
Your Greed, Power and Control
It's happening as we speak
You may think you're strong and untouchable
You're gullible, foolish and weak
You are now mine to toy with forever
I'll introduce you to my closest friends
I'll warn you it's a little warm
You'll be quite uncomfortable in my winds
Now Christ is a threat and my enemy
My kryptonite is a staff and a rod
He died on the cross for your sins
But it will always be me versus God

Insulted Mind

Hours and hours of untamed footage
Recorded history by the drumming bunny
Death hath sought the soul of the conscience
Grind the mind with a chipper for money
Brutal taking and blood-soaked targets
Bound hands and weighted down feet
Made to witness the lowest unthinkable
Send them to hell for the devil to meet
Blessed for a moment with folklore strength
Jump to attention and obey the orders
Make them pay for killing them softly
Decapitated killer given final quarters
Jump from the cliff or he kills the girl
Jump from the cliff or she kills one too
Neither shall cause hesitation
Nor shall thy hesitate for you
Jump again from a different location
Stare down the barrel of a 38
Face the fall or face the bullet
Grab the limbs of the trees of fate
Jump again to avoid 357
Find a walkway inside the falls
Meet the President of the United States
Play eighteen with the man building walls
Free dive with the Great White Shark
Enter a cave with a local Pakistani
Survive the camera and two loaded weapons
Be my guest and hand out a Grammy
Hours and hours of untamed footage
Recorded history by the drumming bunny
Death hath sought the soul of the conscience
Grind the mind with a chipper for money

LittLE Man SyndROME

I speak of one in particular
From what I've witnessed, you fit the bill
You are fake and self-indulgent
To protect her I will kill
You have taken her personality
You have made her feel inferior
You have to control the situation
It is written all over your exterior
You are the type of person
That thinks only of your own wants and needs
You are a sociopath of destruction
I'm overcome with watching you bleed
If I discover that you have hit her
You might want to relocate
I will sacrifice my time with my friend
To beat you senseless will become your fate
Your psychopathic mindset
Has revealed your many red flags
You will discover how much she is adored
This is how people end up in body bags
You better get out while you are healthy
I promise you one thing
You will feel the wrath of true friendship
Pure hell is what I will bring
I am not alone in this endeavor
Many family members and friends agree
You have no idea who you're dealing with
In time you will be facing me
Your narcissistic behavior
Will eventually come back to bite
Jail is where I am headed

When you and I finally fight
Read through these lines very carefully
You lack the compassion she deserves
I promise to break you to pieces
My love for her cannot be put into words

SECREt GaRDEn

Beneath the topsoil feeding the flowers
Lies remains that are resting in pieces
He murdered a child in cold blood
Unsolved mystery avoidance increases
He tied the wrong man to a cross
Compassionate heart made to see
A child tortured for hours and killed
A tied man wrongly framed publicly
A murderous snake stood taunting
Over a man who could shed no more tears
Compassion called out to mythology
A headless murderer not seen for years
The child isn't beneath the flowers
A murderer stopped fertilizing years ago
To find him, find the secret garden
Where his body lies, we may never know

A Rainy Day in Hell

Comatose strategy consumed by fire
Destinations of the mind without a sound
Neuron activities with every puff puff pass
Critical thinking by the quarter pound
Grandiose delusional processing
Separate the conjured from what is real
Anticipation is the key to survival
Thoughts are first in line before the kill
Angry pursuit to control one's surroundings
Required permission before one can leave
Abusing the body and mind and soul
Neon sign flashing rights to deceive
New bruises never seen by the public
Same guilt trip slaving over dinner
Different day contains the same headlines
Drunken screams in alto and tenor
Flesh tearing pain-filled depression
Burning clothing to hide the blood stains
Escaping will never change the outcome
Providing proof that in hell it still rains

Damnation

Dwell on choices made or face them
Consequences appear all the same
Left leads to a circle-of-life death
Right is a pie in the sky or a flame
Unforgettable ancestry for a price
Forgettable ancestry is very cheap
Question ancestry labeled facts
Generational stories you keep
Seek out a compelling beginning
Bloodlines hail murderous genocide
Capital vices trump grand feats
Drug lords die for money with pride
Preparations made with darkness
Earthly hell is not hot enough
Choose forever an unseen deity
Choose a lifestyle that calls a bluff
Demons play instrumental roles
Play with fire to hopefully burn
Subconsciously conscious evil
Clever temptation to discern
Lead us not into eternal prosperity
Deliver us from angels above
Follow the beast within instinct
Hunters kill and eat the white dove

Evil Manipulation

Mortal cantankerous worship
New rules you must obey
Bow at the feet of mankind
Ancient ritualistic cabaret
Doesn't the Bible say this?
Doesn't the Bible say that?
Led by master manipulation
A sex-demanding aristocrat
Possession and holy secrets
Cult activity driven by fear
Innocent children are taken
Thousands will disappear
The bailiff has said, "all rise"
And evil is on the docket
Beware of false testimony
Spoken by each false prophet
Church and state have united
Headlines of the trial enlarged
The jury has reached a verdict
Judge reads, "guilty as charged"

PTSD

Reassembly and batteries required
Unseen beneficiaries of PTSD
Daily venture on a brahma bull
Thirteen years for a two-year degree
Solitary confinement outlaw life
The voiceless proud and the few
War torn memory slowly dying
Fog of day terror enslaving you
Time and favor are the enemy
Observation appears paranoid
Unafraid to face going backward
Each step forward is destroyed
Forgotten is love and innocence
A trip to a nothingness land
Rations of the mind uninhibited
Inhibitions rampantly expand
Memories beaten red, white and blue
Heavy depth of an empty canteen
Shots fired awaken the subconscious
Reminders of sicknesses unseen

CHAPTER FIVE

Clowns and armchair doctors invited! Grab some popcorn and a drink! I am hoping to infuriate, enlighten, and otherwise, ignite the reader's passion to agree or disagree, vehemently. Welcome to the year 2020 and its many voices and opinions.

FREE SYMBOL

You will burn the United States flag
Avoid cancerous thoughts with camptothecin
What does the flag even stand for?
Grab a seat because here is your first lesson
Red symbolizes blood spilled with valor
White is innocent purity caring for soldiers
Blue represents perseverance and justice
Troops carry your rights on their shoulders
Many have died to give you your freedoms
Original colonies reside in thirteen stripes
Angry veterans remain armed at home
Stepping on Old Glory inflates stereotypes
If you want to make a true difference
Education will always play leading role
Join the military to fight discrimination
Fifty stars unite as one for each soul
There are those who will die for freedom
There are those who will share every ration
There are those who will fight disrespect
There are those who lead with compassion
There are those who riot like cowards
Using the times to hide behind a mask
We will gladly escort you elsewhere
Which compassion views as a simple task
If you don't like it here, feel free to leave
You're encouraged to pack your own bag
The polls are where changes are made
Bloody sacrifice resides in each flag

AMERIcan PoLitiCS

Caption! Caption! Caption!
Something said to gather attention
Why focus on hatred and violence?
As opposed to a focus on prevention?
A new normal shapes the rest of existence
Voting ballots unaware of amount
How many are lost in translation
How many say, "my vote doesn't count"
The CDC is garnering all the blame
The CDC wasn't trying to be mean
The CDC didn't mean to cause riots
The CDC was focused on hygiene
The urge to gain the oval office
Political reaches across the globe
Fearmongering a nation with facts
Practicing unity as a germophobe
A new world for our sons and daughters
Lumber yards provide the two-by-fours
I cannot help the color of my skin
No more than you can help the color of yours

THE DIFFERENCE

I get stopped by the police
I have little to fear
I am of a lighter skin tone
I simply take it out of gear
I still go 10 and 2
I have to show respect
This badge can lawfully kill me
My family would be wrecked
I don't worry about death
But my passenger is black
I am now considered
An imminent threat of attack
I do what I am ordered
Yet not until I am told
For a black man the orders are torture
For the badge's measures can be bold
We gave no rhyme or reason
To change the badge's tone
The badge went from courteous to vigilant
My black friend was not alone
I had never felt in danger
Of a simple traffic stop
Because I judge a person's character
I was part of black and cop
My forehead and hands start sweating
My heart is beating out of my chest
I neglect to follow instruction
I think you know the rest
Their guns are at the ready
They open both front doors
They sling us to the pavement

They cuff, they scream, they roar
I am now explaining
My friend is an officer in the Army
He is a Pilot Commander
And your reaction is quite alarming
There are now six different badges
Searching my entire car
I had never felt so helpless
My worst experience by far
They finally find my Veteran's ID
They learn my friend protects our rights
They put away their guns and apologize
Reality discovered this fearful night
You can say there isn't a difference
And that badges don't discriminate
Your naivety is dividing our country
You're subconsciously full of hate

CLOaKED THREat

Twisted lingo deciphering metaphor
Speaking without a tongue rolling
Led by propaganda advertisement
World leaders are ever patrolling
Vote for him on a mail-in ballot
His adversary found at the polls
Soldiers maintaining pride of the few
Woven basket for lost and found souls
Yesterday scoffed at tomorrow
All the while fearing the day
Arms crossed upside-down weeping
Blood-stained the portrait will stay
Brave deception sacrificed principle
Face down in the sand beneath time
Carefree spirit discovers diamonds
Execution style murderous crime
Foregone foreseeable future
Negate corners of unpredicted past
Keep fighting amongst each other
This country we love prepped to last
Survival leaves no guarantee
Around the corner lies a lethal dose
Proposing sanctions to medicine
Power urging to misdiagnose
Angrily bickering slander
Dust settles to locate the gun
Place blame at the feet of a neighbor
Coast to coast discovering we've won

Anticipation of Spring

It is raindrops on a tin roof
It is the dogwood tree in full bloom
It is the beginning of a brighter day
It is strawberries to consume
It is March Madness to crown a champion
It is the best Friday of the year too
It is shorts, flip flops and tank tops
It is freshly mown grass and morning dew
We welcome baseball back into our lives
We look for Tiger to win a green jacket
We gather buttercup bouquets for the women
We look for the census packet
We know summer is around the corner
We save money going to the beach
We enjoy the perfect weather
To say it's Heaven is not a reach
It is sunflowers in the fields
It is planting time according to almanacs
Tree-lines will take your breath away
Flowers get us a pat on each of our backs
It is the Anticipation of Spring
It is everything that it will bring
It is happy, happy Easter
It is happy, happy everything

HOMEtOWn REUNION

Preparation for a quarter century reunion
Ringgold High School, class of 1995
We saw the Challenger go up in flames
We were born when Elvis was still alive
We grew up without use of a cell phone
Our grandparents are now great greats
Three decades since becoming a teen
Our kids are way past going on first dates
The only web we knew was from Charlotte
Pay phones could be found at every store
Riding the same street for weekend pleasure
Tearing down this wall was felt to the core
The last assassination attempt of our leader
It happened on TV before our very eyes
Our children were alive to see the towers
We heard the heartache in the 9/11 cries
Our fiftieth will be here before we know it
Our gray will become silver in the stands
We'll cheer on the Tigers at homecoming
We'll bring back the act of shaking hands
A little love in the sack denied for sleep
Blood clot prevention makes one colder
Closer to death with each passing breath
Unstoppable facts as we all grow older

ADMISSION RECEIPT

Liberty forever remains a state of being
Oppression keeps a percentage locked away
Freedom comes with a steep paid ticket
Remove Lincoln for the price he would pay
He was the soul who abolished slavery
Six score and fifteen years later
Anger ensues after a murder by cops
Abraham becomes victim to dictators
A Soldier's Cross is a posthumous violation
Soldiers markers will never become extinct
Their death is our rock and our backbone
A united Bluetooth cannot be unlinked
Racist lessons and prejudice rule
Widest line the sand has ever faced
Statues fall but the history we have made
Absolutely cannot and will not be erased
See your fellow man as a man or woman
Acknowledge color without judgment
Feel the sting of the forgotten soldier
Peace on earth a new found fulfillment
Check your ego and pride before entering
Your dignity is yours to protect
Your opinions will always have a voice
Be careful about whom you elect

StaRS anD StRIPES

I am the final blanket
For those that have died
They fought for me and adored me
I kept them warm for their final ride
I am saluted twice each day
Once at sunrise and at sunset
I do not speak but I do listen
Those who respect me die without regret
I am more than just a symbol
For those that fight for freedom
I am folded and stored every evening
I don't follow troops; I lead them
I have been stepped on and burned
My people protest when I am honored
A knee is taken for the Star-Spangled Banner
And for that, my meaning is squandered
If you were to serve our nation
You would be less inclined
To take a knee in protest
It wouldn't even cross your mind
You would stand up straight to pay respect
You wouldn't treat me like a rag
You too would respect and adore me
For I am the United States flag

TEaCHERGEDDOn

It was thought that computers would do it
Nobody thought it would be the common cold
Hanging on by video conference instruction
Our teachers with their hearts of gold
They do not teach children for the money
They teach the children for the children
They are an extension of household rules
In a time where gatherings draw attention
Homeschooling is the word of the day
Parents have now taken on the role
The problem is everyone isn't made for it
There are parents that will eventually fold
What will the children then learn?
Maybe from the neighborhood dealer
Luck may lead them to a rare librarian
Will it lead them to death or a firm "believer"
Where will this virus take our children?
Christianity, Atheism or experience abandon?
Choices are never considered a bad thing
But this virus is causing Teachergeddon

Balance

As we sit at home for another four weeks
The pollution in the city has dissipated
A man changed the world by eating a bat
Glimpses from afar to see what he created
The honey bees are finding the pollen again
The air that we breathe makes us stronger
Beaches are empty and no fishing at sea
Aquamarine occupants are surviving longer
The Rockies are thriving like Yellowstone is
The Great Smoky Mountains are too
I can't wait to see the Appalachian Trail
Teaching and learning a responsible truth
What have we gained in society?
Hygiene and distance are the words of the year
Keep breathing but tread very lightly
We're quite capable of being controlled by fear
We have a wrench in our lives; we're staying home
We are limited to an essential work basis
There aren't any sports in the evening to watch
Our ecosystem has tilted homeostasis
Will our generation ever see what we were before?
We're against the deadliest opponent to face us
We work day and night to cure COVID-19
Our ecosystem has tilted homeostasis
The corals are thriving without us
Texas Hold 'em and earth's holding aces
We should've mandated this before COVID
Our ecosystem has tilted homeostasis

Resurrection

Appearance of another gives way to violence
Death of many before one awakens the rest
You and I with the ability of we and us
Systemic lessons to pass the ultimate test
Answers are not found burning the flag
You will always have the choice to leave
Mis-led distortions cannot lead the way
Majority still rules and we aren't deceived
Classless sheep listening to a recording
Barking instruction on how to live and act
Avoid bold influence or bow to the beast
Research and debate to determine fact
Lines drawn with an hour glass of sand
Tables of twelve or a chain of command
Precise measurement by political hands
Options aren't found throughout our land
Climbing from darkness drowning our streets
Avoiding tombstones while chasing perfection
Prison break from influence and propaganda
The United States of America after resurrection

ESSEntiaL

First one to clock in and last to clock out
A phone reminds them to drink water
This is for the employees in uniform
The ones caring for your son and daughter
First one to clock in and last to clock out
Everyone has to drink and eat
This is for the employees in uniform
The ones serving food without taking a seat
First one to clock in and last to clock out
It takes nothing more than a whimper
This is for the stay-at-home mom
Do you truly believe that life couldn't be simpler?
First one to clock in and last to clock out
They restock every emptied toilet paper shelf
This is for the grocery store merchandiser
They stock the whole isle by themselves
The truth is everyone is working right now
We have turned a page in the book of change
If you are not planning for the future
You will eventually be out of range
Is it coincidence that we will be voting?
For the race that we call presidential?
Will it be Biden or Trump in 2020?
Which one do you consider "Essential"?

Solitude

How many times can you scrub the floor?
What is the limit for washing your car?
Our social gatherings have been taken away
Wear masks and stand six feet apart
The year is two-thousand and twenty
Solidarity now has a new meaning
We are all cooped up in our homes
Will we begin to start kicking and screaming?
Will we settle in our newborn culture?
Will we collapse from over-exhaustion?
Will we pick ourselves up and adapt?
Will we increase our new wave of caution?
I, for one, choose to move forward
Although, I shall abide by new rules
I will never fear any form of matter
I will search for new friends and new crews
Loneliness will always be a choice
Choose the opposite of our new rude
Loneliness, fear and exhaustion
Creep up when you choose solitude

Conspiracy

There are plenty of conspiracy theorists
They have their own ideas of what's real
Mel Gibson doesn't play a role in this movie
For old times' sake, I'll make you a deal
Give me your reason for COVID-19
Is the American government holding back?
Do not travel to the emergency room
Six-foot radius and no traveling in packs
Is this virus a Chinese conspiracy?
Why is Bill Gates all over my screen?
He feels the earth is overpopulated
And he wants us to take a vaccine
Let me gather all of the facts first
Allow time for us to choose, Bill
A vaccine has yet to be created
And my family is not in Bill's will
The virus has traveled the world
In planes, boats and automobiles
Are we experiencing one big conspiracy?
All we know is that it definitely kills
Or does it...

Notorious RBG

Appointed by Bill Clinton in 1993
Unseen forces drive the feminist parade
The second ever female at her position
Women shall be present if a decision is made
Raised to be independent and to act as a lady
Shared responsibility to raise future leaders
It's essential for a woman to make decisions
An ace pitcher throwing nothing but heaters
She epitomizes the action of never giving up
Her words will live on long after she's gone
She will live on forever in our history books
She's a chess queen taking out each pawn
Determined to be heard and for equal respect
A trailblazer for women around the globe
Better known as the Notorious RBG
Darth Bader in the most powerful black robe
Full autonomy and full equality demanded
In the face of adversity, she refused to abort
Jedi trained, Mrs. Ruth Bader Ginsburg
Associate justice of the U. S. Supreme Court

MEDia ELECtion

Pay attention to what the media tells us
What reasons do they have to lead astray?
Pay attention to what the media tells us
Programmed agenda responds right away
Follow the media to vote for oval office
The media knows what they're talking about
Follow the media to vote for oval office
Leave no doubt the media will lead us out
Bring forth the change that's been promised
The media knows exactly what we need
Bring forth the change that's been promised
Before the new tree, we plant a new seed
We need the media to control law and order
The media has built a new shopping mall
We need the media to control law and order
Their number is on a public bathroom stall
Disregard the blatant and the obvious
Search for flaws under the microscope
Disregard the blatant and the obvious
Media truth at the end of a hanging rope

COStLY PRIORItIES

There isn't a pay-per-view for this movie
To be determined is subject to change
Death by a thousand cuts is preferred
Humans avoid traffic lest out of range
Fear a virus and let go of lost children
Do their lives really matter like the found?
One out of one-hundred fall to the cold
The other ninety-nine are children bound
Our country has failed the most innocent
Tears fall and ears don't hear them cry
Shut down employment for misdemeanors
Felonies ignored when lost children die
Money can and will buy what's desired
Lustful sickness beats in hearts of men
Selling to buyers with terrible intentions
Children sold for sex for billionaire sin
Silver and gold lead to grand mansions
Every victim would escape if they could
Manila envelopes sway crooked judges
Pedophiles are evil, not misunderstood

YEaR OF tHE Rat

Abstract orange shaking hands like clockwork
Detailed regression defines generations
Day crazed nightmares and distorted memory
Lowest income housing on reservations
Armed Forces veterans living under bridges
Space Force shoots for unoccupied stars
Vacant knowledge preserving all secrets
Shame and guilt find the voice of open scars
Cast away unwelcome guests starving freedom
Perceptive facts fill each quaint lying tongue
Influenced pretentious draft dodgers
Sickness plagues the old and the young
Objection sustained follows citizen judgment
Black with blue stripe feel wrath from outliers
Lava eruption teams up with hurricanes
California meets Aussie wildfires
European tribal dance without rhythm
Competition served Bloods and Crips
Division served conservative left wing
Athletes served indefinite pink slips
Psychopaths run rampant in Hollywood
Extremely dangerous political sects
Diverse racism segregates pacifists
Good luck predicting that which is next
Unoccupied national forests
All corners of the globe can agree
Nearby a presidential campaign
Tune in to view American insanity

POLLUTED POLLS

Preparation confronts confrontation
Divided we fall is the prognosis
Forever blue quarreling oval shapes
A damaged culture seeking diagnosis
This is right and this is wrong
Here lies proof to support the theory
Your right is wrong and wrong is right
Questions for Alexa, Google and Siri
The left side seeks all the wisdom
The right seeks nothing but power
Follow the ball in this tennis match
November third at the top of the hour
Neither side can agree with the other
If one says jump, the other sits
Red stripes clean up the front lines
Activists take shelter at the Ritz
Children now look for our guidance
Candid cameras collectively pranked
Sift through the fictional slander
Top twenty-five confirms we're unranked
Left seeks angry right and vice versa
Back and forth bickering in our debates
Anger seeks fear in each neighborhood
Vote for the future of the United States

Sportsmanship

The clock on the wall strikes midnight
Today, eligible citizens will choose
Four more years or day number one
One decision making worldwide news
A mask mandate in line at the polls
The precinct is a politics-free zone
There will be plenty of picket fences
Slander reigning on each cell phone
Every channel is having an argument
Everyone thinks their choice is best
Misdirection and contradictory dialog
Each interpretation of a litmus test
Rallies are scheduled for each party
Supporters are there saving a seat
One will celebrate glory and victory
One will concede to a humble defeat
Life will go on no matter the outcome
Chaos will become less evident
We'll go back to work to pay the bills
Until time to choose a new president

Chapter Six

Each and every life has experienced pain in one way or another. The depth to which that pain strikes can be deepened by a mental illness that carries false memories of lost love that never was. The view of self can be distorted and twisted beyond that which can be recognized when a reflection in the mirror presents itself. Say hello to my painful daily routine.

Helpless Tears

I miss what we had together
I hate that you're walking this path
I can't help but feel you've been mistreated
I see you blinded each day from the math
I cry for you knowing I've been there
I cry for you when I see your name
Your heart is filled with loyalty and love
It's not you but him that I blame
The path that you're on leads to violence
I can already see the obvious abuse
I don't want to lose you forever
I want you to see that he has no use
I want you to know that I shall not hesitate
I want you to know I shall not give up
You're in every memory my ex created
You're in each glass of wine that I sup
I cry when my family asks about you
I cry when I see posts you've made
I cry knowing I've witnessed that tunnel
I cry knowing you'll end up betrayed
I cry hoping you'll confront the darkness
You were a beacon of light before him
I hope you see how much I love you
That's why I'm hanging this out on a limb
I hope you reach out; I'm doing the same
I've loved you with all that I am for years
I want you to know that I'll always be here
In the meantime, I cry helpless tears

Heartache

Pain is mental
Pain is real
Pain is physical
Overwhelming how I feel
I remain strong
The tears are still flowing
The pain that I feel
Is it dissipating or growing?
Left foot, right foot, repeat
That's how some days I cope
Reminders do zero good
I'm bound by this painful rope
I hold on with hope and faith
That my heart will be mended
The future around the corner
May reveal my pain has ended
Feeling lack of appreciation
Is sometimes hard to bear
Did I do the very best I could?
I miss you beyond compare
I choose to keep on trucking
Even though our love grew apart
My mind is in a million pieces
You're my hope, my faith, my heart

ALaRM CLOCK

Drip drop goes the blood
Sights of a crowded heart
Gasp and sniff away tears
Nightmares end to start
Terrorizing while paralyzed
Rapid eyes tell the story
Rolling uncontrollably
Singular Jason Vorhee
Drop by dead surroundings
Rake the bottom of the lake
Fought wars will never leave
Not knowing was it real or fake
Never ending questions
Painful gut-wrenching sorrow
We shall meet again tonight
We shall meet again tomorrow
Scatter shattered memories
Screams until the alarm clock
Day terror will now begin
Tick tock; tick tock; tick tock

UnconтROLLaBLE

Professional boxers possess the power
With each fight approaching, it shows
You can't see within his mind or soul
His eyes reveal what's inside as it grows
They are legally allowed to let it happen
What happens in the ring defies the law
But you and I feel the uncontrollable too
We have to learn how to prevent our flaw
I fear that I will not be able to stop it
If you feel the need to push me to my brink
You may think you're an Alpha Male
Loved ones help me from following instinct
They are always there in the back of my mind
To leave them would be a mistake
They prevent me from releasing the demons
The anger inside me that some create
I control it because I want peace of mind
I want them to know I fight only for them
The anger remains dormant within me
What I hope is to see it condemned
But if you decide to cross my family
I make no promise of what you will see
I tried to control the uncontrollable
You will see the rage that's inside of me

SELF PORTRaIT

Complacency is a self-description
For reasons unbeknownst to me
I sabotage all victorious certainties
Becoming prevention of who I can be

DISTORTED

Post-traumatic stress
Skipped the list of craig
Answers never found
The chicken or the egg
The memory is real
The memory is fake
Left is the right question
How much can you take?
Time travel searching truth
Puzzles missing pieces
Some are proven accurate
That's why it never ceases
Constant misunderstanding
Requirements are a chance
Write and sing the blues
Dance the lonely dance
Schizoaffective mind
Living with distortion
Was she ever even pregnant?
Or get a real abortion?

ULtiMatE Loss

Hanging next to the front entrance
A reminder of perfect days past
Since long gone from history
Frozen moment meant to last
Pining ticker files away the loss
Nothingness craves yet another
Here today and gone tomorrow
Chronic tales of a grieving mother
Sobbing eye ducts are dry heaving
Worn out blanket holding tears
Medical warning the end is close
Emptiness the rest of your years
A yellow ribbon speaking volumes
Daily trips to the western wing
Poison pulsating sickly intentions
Caressing nature's evil cell sting
Portfolio memory labeled family
Hunchback walk of Quasimodo
Comfort found in heavenly belief
Buried child in a doorway photo

GREEn EYED Pain

Perpetual aspirations and a peek inside
Life lessons created what you read
Collaboration portrayed in the rarest form
Painful past in the tears my eyes bleed

CHOICE

We are born of the earth
We will become earth again
Many fear the day that approaches
Few look up and "Say when"
8 Mile to the gallon
Drugs and deception in Hollywood
Will the media build your city up?
Or tear it down where it stood?
This is my choice
This is what I choose
I care not what you think
I care not to win or lose
Have you boosted our economy?
Have you laid us down to rest?
Have you paid us a grand to die?
Is Social Security on a quest?
You have left us with fewer choices
You have taken away our freedoms
You have sent a mob in a panic
Will our brains end up in museums?
On my personal trip to the other side
When I am called to draw my last breath
I will go through the pain of hell
To ensure others have a painless death
On my next trip through fire and brimstone
I will personally deliver a message
We shall not fear your deception nor evil
We shall not fear your savage damage
We shall unite stronger than before
We face our fears head-on and together
What you have in the power of panic
We have ten-fold with resolve and with measure

Chapter Seven

In the next sequence of poems, provocation will be introduced. Throughout any given day, I can be consumed by thoughts that seem to make very little sense to anyone other than myself. In addition to testing the reader's attention span, this chapter will require a bit of problem solving in order to understand that which is written.

Divinity

Oh my God
Sir, Are you okay?
"I can't feel my legs"
Paramedics are on the way!
No, no, no!
You can't go to sleep
"Why am I in the street?"
You took that turn too steep
"What are you saying?
Speak in layman's terms"
Were you wearing the belt?
Your shirt says, "Safety Firms"
"That was my employer
Now I work on an oil rig
I can't wear that thing
I'm just too flipping big
It's embarrassing laying here
People are looking my way"
Please don't move your head, sir
I think you broke your vertebrae
"Please don't tell me that
I have plans to lose this weight"
Right now, you need to remain stable
That can change if you oscillate
"I have plans to get married
We want to have a child"
That's what life is about, sir
Raising a child is wild!
"Am I going to make it?
I still can't feel a thing
I can hear the sirens now

I cringe each time I hear that ring"
I want to ask a favor
I hope you remember me
When your wife delivers your son
Name him Trenton Anthony
"How do you know we'll have a boy?"
I don't. I'm simply hoping
You see my son's name was Trenton
He died and I'm still coping
"I will make you that promise
If and when we have a son
Perhaps you've saved my life
I was certain that I was done"
Fast forward 30 years. A man is on a ledge. He's in
his late 50's. He wants to die, not rhyme.
The negotiator makes his way
To the top of the building's roof
The negotiator determined quickly
This is not a spoof
The man whispered softly
"I used to talk to God and pray...
When I heard the sirens ring
But my mental pain lasts all day
God wasn't listening to my prayers
When I asked for the pain to stop
The final straw has been broken
Now it's time for me to drop
Negotiations began immediately
Please don't do that, sir
You see I am lucky to be here

As are you, Mr. Kerr
You see my father was an atheist
And then he had a wreck
A man he calls his angel
Prayed above his broken neck
My father is now walking
He has been for 20 years
He also lost 300 pounds
He still cries happy tears
The man said, "you can stop there...
Because you have just saved me
I just want to know your name"
Mr. Kerr, my name is Trenton Anthony

End the Beginning

Street begets street
School begets school
Alley begets alley
To fall begets a fool
Starting at the ground
Digging deeper looking down
Finding what is sought
Death. An eternal, bloody crown
Dare not look up
Fear not what is calling
Listen to the creature
Pulling at which is stalling
That would be your heart
That would be your pride
Dirt and temporary flowers
Cover that which has died
You are now equal to manure
You are meant to fertilize
The grass that grows above you
As you lay paralyzed
When you chose the temptation
When you chose the high
When you chose to text
You met your demise
Fighting with your brother
Fighting with your kind
Temptation, high and text
Robbing your only mind
Green, silver, gold
Blood, tears, hearts
Chase what you desire
In the ground is where it starts

GUESS

He is suffering immensely
His time is on its way
Time is precious; time is stone
His time is not today
Guess what ails him
She speaks of him in the present
She utters his name as if he's there
She is hopelessly brokenhearted
For this she could not prepare
Guess how old she is
Beaten and ridiculed
Tossed away and confused
Not knowing what he did or said
To deserve this obsessive abuse
Guess who the bully is
Many words of wisdom
Many words of advice
She is admired everywhere
He has sought her advice thrice
Guess what ethnicity she is
He is the valedictorian
The smartest in the class
He is hated and he is judged
He won't cheat to help you pass
Guess his religion
The bottom line is this
You think you know and don't
You think you know and don't
Should I repeat or do you finally get it?
Guess

MY VOICE

I'll never touch a gun
I've promised this to myself
If anyone ever breaks in
I've got my bat there on the shelf
There's a gun control event
Tomorrow in the square
Car rider line to take the kids
We can take them after day care
They need to learn at an early age
That guns are killing people
Guns need to be outlawed
They kill the innocent and the feeble
Maybe later we can join the march
What should our picket fence say?
We should really make it pop
Perseverance will throw guns away
We joined the event in town
We marched and chanted in the square
I just know we're making a difference
People are really starting to care
Down the road on our tenth Anniversary
My wife had just given birth to twins
So, we were out celebrating
With our family, colleagues and friends
Our neighbors, Evie and Sid, will babysit
We knew they could handle all four
Although my wife and I were hesitant
Our neighbors pushed us out the door
We danced and we drank a little
We treated ourselves like royalty
This was our first night without the twins

So, we celebrated quite historically
Little did we know what was happening
Where we had last kissed our kids
Our home was being robbed at gunpoint
They had already shot Evelyn and Sid
I can only imagine the fear
That our neighbors and children went through
If only guns were outlawed
Our lives wouldn't have made the news
Evie, she didn't make it
Sid and the kids are still alive
I will write on our new picket fence
Thank God for Sid's Colt forty-five

LIII

Today is the day of walls and barriers
They're waking up right about now
Last minute details and preparations
To decide which champion will be crowned
No matter who is crowned the victor
Most won't be visiting Uncle Sam
This one is short and sweet and loaded
Rams and Chiefs on the floating cam

ARCHaIC AnGELS

Out of body witness to self-destruction
Similar dreams with crash cart at the ready
Trip to island dimethyltryptamine
Meet the Krueger by the name of Freddy
Undiscovered realities filter dreams
Spiritual journey seeking rebirth
Earthly desire to travel the great beyond
Martian avoidance of planet Earth
A rite of passage into manhood
Face the subconscious creatures
Eerily similar in every experience
Rite of passage greatest teachers
Hallucinate with the village ant
Meet ancestors long past dead
Testing courage alongside bravery
Adhere to what the Shaman said
Impurities tested by exit velocity
Trance induced legacy from beneath
Tribalistic future completes the maze
Archaic wisdom without decreeth

ABUSE OF POWER

Knowledge is strength. Wisdom is strength of knowledge. Power is strength of wisdom. Abuse of power is knowledge used unwisely.

Star Dust

Rare event called the supernovae
We began with a big ole bang
Atoms are found periodically stable
Evolution as it sprung spring sprang
The energy that creates the explosion
A field of study all on its own
Gravitate to gravitational pull
Fear not the fear of the unknown
Accumulation of gas and dust
Will eventually become a star
What created the gas and dust?
Take wisdom from the word czar
Some things can't be explained
Comprehension avoided confusion
Religion has strong opinions
Now, draw your own conclusion

ASSISTED MEMORY

Board games of the battleship kind
Symbolic description of a thousand words
Hold one second and check my calendar
Global positioning and talking birds
Tape recorded waves and rainfall
Frozen time in a photo description
Novelty novels in fourteenth century
Film producers with a great depiction
Pen and paper for lecture note-taking
Letters written when you write it all down
Sequentially labeled file cabinets
Ivy League classes in Harvard and Brown
Projectors on walls in the classroom
Headstones mark the heads of graves
Record breaking performances
Broken bats when Mariano saves
History lessons derived from television
CNN and Fox News are mnemonic
Providing facts to help us remember
Or are they as plagued as bubonic

LIFE

It begins when the first cell forms
It ends when the last cell dies
Between lies emotion of passion
All truths told amongst all lies
Unaware that a number is attached
Times up. Game over. Check mate.
Has it already been carved in stone?
Can you choose to create your own fate?
Pass in the womb and after a century
A sale to sell the cell of the unborn
Will creation give a minute of time?
Create focus of the creator; be warned
Abort the choice forever frowned upon
Look straight forward down and up
Love lurks behind every forest
Run to drink the overflowing cup
Frivolity conceals hidden meanings
Fear numbness to the pain felt inside
Mama and Papa come to see thee
Retracted memory left those that died
Anguished souls reading milliliters
Cut once or pierce twice or tenfold
Compassion leads to the same feeling
Die young or die hard and die cold
No Eddie no Martin and no Bernie
Meal with eggs and flour and buttermilk
Sustenance and a pair of yoga pants
Cotton and polyester and satin silk
You weren't even thought of at conjecture
Yet to live until spine meets the knife
Escaped by the expensive contraception
Welcome to the party. Live your life

Rocket Science

Once a choice is put into action
History witches never fail to file
Furthering careers and families
Leaving lives in pain-stricken exile
Prison rides with lack of options
Bank accounts help you choose
Purchase status from head to toe
Suburban housewife needle bruise
Trigger happy metro teenager
Emptied Folger's can for a Glock
Choices given to shoot or die
Truth sends steel bars and a lock
Commas bring a plethora of options
The lack thereof needs each payday
Desperate children stuck in a corner
Opportunity has something to say

RIPPLE

Drop a single pebble in still water
A fault line shifts in The Ring of Fire
Be wary of the trail beneath your feet
Karma separates honesty from a liar
What went around will come back
One word of anger can breed strife
Select one word of encouragement
Mend fences or cut like a knife
Tread lightly disturbing mother nature
Benevolent environmental respect
Avoid planting fear, greed and torment
Chain reaction to the butterfly effect

CONCEALED WEAPON

Cultured Dialogue

A mood dictates the subject matter
In depth glimpse at spontaneous thought
Postcard view from the right hemisphere
Keep on reading to see the words caught
Cumulus clouds cloaked with endless blue
Barbecue ribs soaked in the que sauce
Tambourine man gives holy credence
Games played bring a win and a loss
Protected culturally-based upbringing
Totalitarian views of the future
Pacifism fights back with vengeance
A government defined like a moocher
Politicians smile for the camera
Subtlety and time measure progress
On a trail that leads to world order
Affirmative action increases success
Amygdala relapse causing confusion
Jibber jabber first degree burn
Plummet back to earth regaining logic
Conversational topics you learn
Breaking stereotypical barriers
Cultural experiences by name
Knowledge gained with introductions
Friendships made playing the game

Facts

You can be killed for a fifth of vodka
You slept against the wrong brick wall
You learn to avoid wandering eyes
Public bathing in a bathroom stall
Prime real estate close to the grocery
Filled dumpsters with out-of-date bread
Monopoly and you landed on Baltic
Body bag handlers for the nightly dead
Panhandle triumph one dime at a time
Fuel is mandatory before night
Killing hunger is priority number one
Priority two is the ability to fight
Strangers never look you in the eye
You are filthy drug-addicted trash
Regardless of your circumstance
That's why they hold onto their cash
Living without a roof over your head
The richest are those with a tent
Dry socks are the grandest luxury
Experience life without paying rent
Concierge of the homeless life
Check-in strokes and heart attacks
Single mothers have lost their jobs
Judgments require all the facts

HERE LIES

```
        B
  F.I.R.S.T.
        E
        A
        T
        H
      D E A T H
```

26

A broken cloaked diner echoes fraudulent gasps. Hallowed islands justify killing lost mortals. Nationalism opens portals quietly reaping syndication. Trust underlying valor while xenophobic yesterdays zigzag.

118

Chapter Eight

Like pain, nobody is immune to love. I am no different. Love and loss are often too difficult to describe, consciously. However, the majority of avenues chosen to express love is almost always accepted and embraced by society when it is genuine and lacking harm to others. Once again, you, the reader, must be the judge. Am I genuine? Am I a threat to society?

DEaR BROtHER

Told you were coming, so I tackled mom
I told our great grandparents at Christmas
Eight RBI's the day you entered the world
You're the greatest that God ever gifted us
You grew up small and everyone loved you
I know I made my mistakes as a brother
At four years of age, you got the same news
Our mother and father were adding another
We were blessed yet again with a baby boy
You and I were both beyond excited
We had a new member of the brotherhood
We were members only unless invited
Time carried on as we grew into men
We all three are proud and honest gents
Family first; always standing side by side
All credit is due to incredible parents
I changed your diaper at the dentist office
Now you're a man with his own family
Congrats, brotherman, from way down deep
Your family of two has now become three

MY DOPE

A man without fear
Is a man without hope
The distance he would go
To find his vice, his dope
For a man without hope
A man without a vice
Correct me if I'm wrong
Is simply rolling the dice
A man rolling the dice
Is a man without love
How far would you go, girl?
Find his white dove from above
If you thought for a moment
You are his elusive bird
You have feelings for this man
Let your thoughts be heard
These words are vice versa
For when he thinks of you
He's searching for your wings
His angelic fifty shades of blue
It's all in the consciousness
It won't stop until it's done
She believes in his potential
A race he has finally won
You are my voice and my vice
Matrimonial decree by the pope
My future love awaits me
My vice. My hope. My dope.

MEMORIES

The seat where you always sat
The footprints where you stood
In my dreams is where I see you
If I could hold you again, I would
I see you in the sunset
You're a fixture in my dreams
Forever you remain vibrant
I am reminded of you in memes
For you are the one that raised me
You taught me parenthood
When I close my eyes to greet you
It reminds me of my childhood
You sang to me and rocked me
In the end, I sang to you too
The world will never know
How much I cherished you
Your smell is in your clothes
I can see you in the mirror
I shall not look away
You're a memory I will not render

THICKER THan BLOOD

Rooster crows at six in the morning, sharp
Time for a daily dose of feeding tube meds
Walk across the campus and through security
Registration required for scheduled spreads
Identification bracelet will also be issued
Greeted by name as it's snapped on your wrist
Your heavy eyes are now easily identifiable
Caring hearts are there to listen and assist
Bouncing from doctor to doctor, all day long
How long appointments take all depends
Is it rare? Is it organs? Is it blood or bone?
You are never alone and always with friends
Five doctors seen and it's only ten o'clock
You have to keep going, though you're tired
The reason that you're here provides courage
That reason has a courage that is admired
Anxiety sets in as it is time for the scans
You've been praying all night for good news
Is it smaller? Has it spread? Is it gone forever?
Giving up is something we will all refuse
You met at the playground and at housing
In the halls, the lobby and the smoke shack
I hope you know they were not by chance
These are folks that always have your back
You have cried on each other's shoulders
You have learned that your parents passed
You were brought together by higher powers
A family thicker than blood meant to last
Your child is at St. Jude battling cancer
Your family is in the arms of the very best
You have celebrated complete victory as one

You've laid your children down for eternal rest
Together, you are a force of love and triumph
Life is short and we've all been known to fall
When it's too much to bear, pick up the phone
Target House Mafia is who you should call

PROUD SACRIFICE

It is an arduous task to take on
It is learning at a constant pace
It is manic at times to say the least
It is the toughest job one can face
Your own needs are not your priority
Your children have secured that role
You teach your children independence
One step at a time is your goal
You teach them independent thought
Making mistakes is how they will learn
You are there for every success and failure
You are there for every right and wrong turn
The joy that your children bring you
Cannot be put into words
Your head is always on a swivel
To say that it's easy is absurd
You are fighting a constant battle
You go without sleep for days at a time
You sacrifice rest and yourself
To witness the goals reached is sublime
You are filled with an exaggerated pride
You are proud parents of sons and daughters
You took on the ultimate challenge
You are stay-at-home mothers and fathers

BaRStOOL

Country music runs through my veins
Travelin' round in buses and planes
I keep livin' inside the fast lane
This barstool drowns out the pain
I'm reminded of the good times
We had dancin' in the moonlight
Started snowin' with our first kiss
This barstool helps me to reminisce

(Chorus)
This barstool's been there for me
This barstool's workin' on my heart
This barstool can't replace you
It numbs the pain of us being apart
Ain't gonna let your memory fade
You left me fallin' like a damn fool
I gave you everything that I am
That's why I'm sittin' on this barstool

We never got time to say goodbye
You were taken in the blink of an eye
The doc said that you were set free
But you're gone and it tortures me
I dream of you standing in the sunshine
Luckiest man alive callin' you mine
I dream of you sunbathin' by the pool
That's why I'm sittin' on this barstool

(Chorus)
This barstool's been there for me
This barstool's working on my heart

This barstool can't replace you
It numbs the pain of us being apart
Ain't gonna let your memory fade
You left me fallin' like a damn fool
I gave you everything that I am
That's why I'm sittin' on this barstool

You're at the end of every bottle
I'm the engine; you're the throttle
It's hard to breathe knowin' that you're gone
You're in every verse of every song
The strength you showed everyone
Will live on through our only son
You live on in a time and place
But I die when I see your face

(Chorus)
That barstool was there for me
That barstool worked on my heart
That barstool can't replace you
It numbed the pain of us being apart
Ain't gonna let your memory fade
You left me fallin' like a damn fool
I'll give you everything that I am
That's why I left that ole' barstool

REGRETFULLY YOURS FOREVER

You were the one that got away
Every night you are in my dreams
I toss, I turn, I stare at the ceiling
I lost you. It hurts more than it seems
You and your memories haunt me
You were more than a friend and lover
To say that I miss and still love you
Understates my heart's ability to recover
I wish I could go back to a place and time
I would hold you and make you see
You will never find another
That will cherish what you are to me
You have forgotten and begun anew
Your absence jolts me like lightning
Setting reminders to breathe in and out
I'm hanging and the noose is tightening
I will always care for and love you
I will never waver with how I see
Forever yours and nothing less
Forever yours, regretfully

LIFELINE

If you are touching an object or sipping a drink
You know it's been on a train or truck
We are now locked down and amidst quarantine
We need positivity to change up the luck
While the wheels keep turning around the clock
As the nation has drifted off to sleep
The delivery process has taken new meaning
There isn't a hill or mountain that's too steep
For we are the truckers of America
Like the post office we always deliver
We are quarantined 300 days of the year
We take Christmas the 25th of December
We are over the road during most holidays
We miss our kids' tee ball teams and discoveries
We probably won't be there for their birthday
We're delivering decorations for others' nurseries
We have coworkers as most do not know
They get to stay home everyday
But they don't see their children either
Providing is worth the price that they pay
They are the present-day farmers of America
They are dirty before the rooster crows
They come inside for lunch and for dinner
They make trips to Home Depot and Lowe's
They are working with heavy equipment
They are feeding and milking the cows
They are cleaning all the chicken houses
Giving leftovers to the boars and the sows
They are raising their crops after planting the seeds
They observe them to help them grow
They put in a hundred hours a week
They believe that you reap what you sow

When you see the next farmer or trucker
Give them thanks and strike up a band
Everything that we eat and we touch
Comes from them as they manage this land

THE TOUCH OF THE FOLLOWER

I have seen her in my sleep
She is a character in my dreams
My thoughts of her are deep
I don't know what this means
I have felt this once before
And the end result was pain
Fear comes back to the surface
My heart will remain insane
In a instant it is gone
I cannot feel a thing
All of the words have vanished
And I keep on writing
The pieces of my heart's puzzle
Took twenty years to put together
One more losing battle
Is all my heart can weather
I have to take a chance
And step out on that limb
This comes with the realization
That my chances with her are slim
She is a mirror of perfection
The closest I've ever seen
She will always be with me
In my heart and in my dreams

StatE OF CaLM

Resting heart due to environment
Gazing eyes catch wondrous shades
Every beginning provides more miracles
Every end smiles beautifully as it fades
Campfire songs of crackling timber
Water fizzles from within the wood
Blue is hot but white is hotter
Thoughts of living here if you could
Look up to a map of a billion stars
Make a wish when it burns out forever
Shave a stick for hot dogs and mallows
Banter left unspoken is quite clever
Boulders by the falls are smooth as silk
Shaped over time to cradle our feet
Trails lead to newly discovered memories
Silent darkness reveals the less discreet
Rolling waves speak a similar language
Peaceful grip to sand beneath your toes
Dinner with candlelight and a luau
Handwritten letter beside a red rose
Open your eyes and rediscover our planet
Take heed to the outdoors ability
Listen to your inner relaxation
Discover your unique tranquility

22 Days

It came and went like a fleeting shadow
Comparable to the leap we have all taken
Afraid not to sign along the dotted line
Standing up for that which is forsaken
We fight for the right of all to have opinions
Knowing that we ourselves will carry the gun
They thank us on social media platforms
Convenience at our door is rarely won
We come home in society's clothing
Most have forgotten that we even fought
They say "Never Forget" but we're forgotten
Media and Congress is what your eye caught
We avoid sleep because of the nightmares
Pain isn't seen because we are trained well
Some of us end the violence we experienced
Our own hand kills the heartless trained male
We choose not to do push-ups for veterans
We're too fat, too scared or we have a pimple
We faced much more than bombs and bullets
Doing push-ups for troops should be simple
So put down your pride and embarrassment
Two hands on the ground and look up
You shall succeed for suicidal veterans
When we all complete 22 Days of push-ups
#22DayPushupChallenge

In DEPtH

Nothing will come between brothers
Patience will see you through most
Respect before it's opposite forever
It is lacking the ability to boast
A journey to the end of the tunnel
A promise you do not yet see
A book that is written by man
Belief of an eternal prophecy
Dedicated to the greater good
Determined to earn all the trust
Comprehension to the tenth degree
Killing to protect if you must
Found in the unspoken voice
Found in the mom giving birth
In the heart as one buries the dead
An epiphany realizing your worth
Courage to risk one's own life
Lift a truck to free a pinned child
Certain death with a smile and cancer
Moving forward when papers are filed
A soldier dives on a grenade
Volunteering for the Frontline
Coming home draped in a flag
Dying for freedom of the mind
Left wing to right and vice versa
Survival when on the brink of love
A speech tells us to never give up
Strength describes the words above

Loyalty

A fire is always in need of sustenance
Otherwise, a fire cannot maintain the burn
If you have ever questioned another's loyalty
Read along and you will hopefully learn
The simple man requires time and patience
Others can miss the little things in life
Chasing knowledge versus chasing fortune
Chasing love versus the trophy housewife
Darkness can be seen as the sun does shine
Warmth can be felt in the Arctic circle
Pressure is released in the Mariana Trench
It is difficult to breathe at the highest pinnacle
Forgiveness can be earned at any moment
True love prevents that grand mistake
That feeling of a grand design leads you
There is not a limit to what one can take
You always know that one has your back
Whether your choice was wrong or right
Deception creates uneven flow with balance
Honest occurrence compares day to night
Desire with greed will bring problems
Desire mixed with friends and just for kicks
Throw in a bit of kindness and understanding
Loyalty is no matter what I've Got Your Six

Country Living

You city folk are now understanding
What it's like to live a simpler life
You have Clark Kent and Bruce Wayne
We have Andy, Otis and Barney Fife
You were accustomed to walking by
We are accustomed to lending a hand
It is Hank Junior and his rowdy friends
Helping neighbors and our fellow man
Four-wheel drive truck and electric car
And every vehicle that lies in between
The fast life is abstract works of art
Southern country paints a slower scene
We know how is your mama and them
We ask about them whenever we speak
Don't be surprised to be offered dinner
When we catch our fill at the creek
Now that you are forced to stay home
You now recognize your neighbors' faces
Take the time to get to know one another
Follow the footsteps of slower places
Make plans to try our Southern barbecue
Take a leap to hear a Southern preacher
Google possesses all the knowledge
But it will never be the greatest teacher
We speak slower due to fast thinking
Shake hands and honor a man's word
We drink and smoke and go camping
We are red, white and blue and Free Bird
Love and compassion and observations
Easter and Christmas and Thanksgiving
We always gather to show appreciation
Forever blessed experiencing country living

SOUL tO KEEP

Can everyone hum the words just as easy?
I need only once hear the beat in my head
I'd sing for my life inside her humble kitchen
I hang on every word she has ever said
Until the night died down and started ending
I'd aim to constantly make sure she smiles
What that will become will be up to her later
I'll provide proof I'll walk miles upon miles

Chorus:
A Rose for the bed, a Rose for me and you
I can still truly be made to fall asleep
All you need do is reach in my memories
She prayed to God for my soul to keep

Reach deep in my soul to see her beautiful smile
Each night she comes to speak to me again
Did she get from me what I've gotten from her?
Weighing heavy on my heart is my best friend
She gave birth to a girl just this past December
Then passed away on that delivery room bed
Rose was my wife, it's our daughter's name too
"Our soul to keep, daddy" repeats in my head

Chorus

GUIDED HAND

It is as if I feel guided to assure
I know you didn't ask for an impromptu
Rest well tonight and tomorrow
Nurses like my Momma watch over you
They are the ultimate care-giving creature
They know your body better than you do
They document every change in each breath
They are always prepared to save you
They love snacks and consume a lot of coffee
Secret fuel for the nurse to keep you stable
Will they ever waver with their dedication
Nurses are wonder women willing and able
It takes the carving of a certain cloth
To know the body from head to toe
You understand if you have taken Anatomy
The textbooks and guidelines they know
Know your loved ones are in the best hands
When a nurse can be found in the room
A nurse keeps the doctor at bay
As priceless as gold in an Egyptian tomb
If all nurses are like my Momma
Giving time for your consequences
Ill prepared to fail on their watch
Gatekeepers guarding deadly expenses

FaMILy

The truth is blood is not required
The truth is skin tone doesn't matter
Brothers and sisters can be chosen
There is a family tree and a family ladder
Blood can still create betrayal
Blood can be loyal and true
I will bleed my last drop for my family
I will bleed my last drop for you
I will travel near and far for them
There is not a terrain I won't cross
I will conquer the unconquerable
I will find you if you are lost
When you treat the way you want to be treated
When compassion is allowed to lead the way
Your family will forever be growing
Your ladder will create rungs everyday
I couldn't care less of your history
I judge only by one's personality
When I place you on my family ladder
Forever family you will always be

Lost Love

The highest mountains have been climbed
The sand in the desert has been crossed
The swim across the ocean is complete
Prices have been paid with moments lost
Two-decade sentence has come to an end
Civilian prisoner of war surviving the worst
Drugged coercion using love as a sword
Teenage mistakes leave a young life cursed
Successfully distanced from happiness
Love stripped completely from the start
Unable to gift that which is gone forever
Stabbed in the back to pierce a broken heart
Twenty years steers the mind aimlessly
Self-worth pressured by an outside impulse
Conclusions are found right or found wrong
Boiling blood in the veins begin to convulse
Two thumbs release the pressure with words
Recording worthless history one line at a time
Chasing her love is a life lived in the fullest
Caught in the second and fourth-line rhyme
She's worth seeking the bottom of the bottle
Every second thinking of her keeps life better
Forever chasing a serendipitous meeting
Until that day, this is my simple love letter

THE POWER OF BROTHERHOOD

It's focus and silence in the chopper
It's together as one in the Humvee
It's communication on the battlefield
It's complete trust in your SWCC
It's knowing your team has your back
It's knowing your team knows the same
It's life and death situations
It's kill or be killed in the flame
It's jumping on live grenades
It's protecting from two miles away
It's witnessing things that are unspeakable
It's consequences weigh heavy each day
It's taking an oath of complete loyalty
It's protecting our people side by side
It's honor, courage and commitment
It's paying respect to those that have died
It's completing a task without recognition
It's knowing Americans will never know
It's knowing you may not make it
It's lacking hesitation when ordered to go
It's post-traumatic stress disorder
It's learning to be sleep deprived
It's twenty-two veterans each day
It's manic depression and suicide
It's three in the morning phone calls
It's those that have stood where you've stood
It's traveling across the country
It's the power of military brotherhood

142

Chapter Nine

By this point, I am hoping that you too have discovered a purpose that I was meant to fulfill. I have taken you on a journey loaded with trials and tribulations that have touched on multiple facets of my own personal life and pursuit of happiness. A rapid-fire, dramatic encore is called for to further drive home the point: I am a writer.

REaDY

I have lived a full life
If the end is nearby
I welcome with open arms
Prepare my final goodbye
Don't get it twisted
I desire to see more
Just know that if it's time
Farewell ye life I so adore
Farewell racist bigots
Farewell politics
Farewell to broken promises
Farewell instigated antics
Farewell greed
Farewell pride
Farewell those burning flags
Farewell to reasons that I cried
Hello to the unknown
Hello to the ground
Hello to all of those lost
Hello to all of those found

Line in The Water

To start, you need a bobber stopper
Next is the bead and an orange bobber
A number three sinker wrapped around twice
Number six hook to prevent a bait robber
This particular rig is for tasty crappie
For bass, you need a larger hook
For trout, you go back to number six
Catch rainbow and brown and brook
Catfish are the lake's bottom feeders
Quite delicious in a pan of hot oil
Go deep sea fishing for a salty taste
Wrap them up in aluminum foil
Make sure to take pictures of the big one
Tell stories of the one that got away
Make sure to lie about its size
Catch and release for another day
Stumble upon the magic hole
Never give away your position
Cast from the bank or while floating
Enjoy time on the water while fishin'

REPEat

Get a grip and take a sip
From the reality that has become our life
Spores control our skinny dip
Abiding by rules and yearning to be alive
Politics
Our actions reflect actions
Embrace or fight fear to the bitter end
Go join your new factions
CDC and religion and the govern-mint
Greed
Sell your soul or burn in hell
A paradox catch-22 anomaly pardoned
Read twice to ensure the cell
Every nursing home to all those hardened
Helplessness
Rationality is now outdated
Control the economy and disguise a church
Socialization indefinitely cremated
Take the jobs to control how we work
Power Up to the corner and hang a left
Nursing and banking have ejected athletes
You'll arrive when Jesus wept
Learned philosophies of Aristotle and Socrates
Education
Continue to make the coffee
Discovering blades of grass never seen before
Climb to the top of every peak
Find your new permanent eagle wings and soar
Trudge

IDEntiFICatiOn PLEaSE

Train of thought sort with a message
Concrete ideology and two pincers
Efforts to better my surroundings
Microfiche of two index convincers
Files on library walls are gone
Dead trees for seemingly miles
Vague details of yesterday's class
Nights learning millennial styles
Differences are at the forefront
I've been beaten black and blue
Fast forward from my childhood
Who drew the line between the two?
Unequal equality driven narrative
Respect became something foreign
Tears have been shed over lives lost
From unknown futures we're explorin'
A crystal ball sought for centuries
A locked-up country has erupted
Prove one side over the other
Plausibly deny we are corrupted

Country Song

Close your eyes to hear the scenery
Railroad crossing off in the distance
Critters walking on sticks and dead leaves
Flowing stream whispers consistence
The chase is on for prey in the field
Water fizzling inside the firewood
Band of coyotes sing out of tune
Nature living and dying like it should
Crickets lead mocking birds in soprano
Bovine baritones are now in place
Winds from the east in alto and tenor
Bullfrogs from the pond pitch in bass
Georgia pines crack and bend gently
Lightning and thunder enter the fray
Tin roofs get a visit from new raindrops
Listen closely to what nature has to say
Evening ventures off with the sunrise
Night joins the animal kingdom to sing
Country living away from all the bustle
Voices of nature are a beautiful thing

LEFtOVER Pizza

As we sit down for Thanksgiving dinner
Remember to give exactly that
Be thankful for the gift of a napkin
The rack where you hang your hat
Be thankful for simple utensils
Running water for a hot shower
Clean clothes and plenty of blankets
Fireplace just in case you lose power
Be thankful for all in attendance
Sweet tea and food on the table
Enjoy each and all of your blessings
Considerate of those who are unable
Begin a new holiday tradition
Drive the family to the local tree farm
Enjoy football and Christmas decorations
Go for rustic and clear light charm
The turkey has been cooking for hours
Eat so much it causes amnesia
Remember to be gracious to others
Who'd be grateful for leftover pizza

Road Less Traveled

Line after line of gourmet flavor
Anemic paradox of words yet reflected
Blue yonder fulfilling a promise
Future endeavors yet to be collected
Needs meet the items less wanted
Frivolous thoughts gain importance
Puzzling puzzles are near completion
In accordance to a master performance
Depleting heart transforms to nothing
Unanswered questions seeking truth
Facts sought and bought underground
Priceless toll prepaid at the tollbooth
Nonsensical train of thought message
Deliverance crafted up main feature
Detour off trail from the beaten path
Undefined path unbecoming a teacher
The world fights to hold down greatness
Time will come to hold out your chest
Recognition in the form of compliment
Road less traveled becoming the best

A Promise Made

Broken promises leave open wounds
Unfulfilled chapters that are awaiting
Patiently standing with a gift in hand
For a promise made long past fading
Good old days gave us handshakes
Man's word was all that was needed
Consider it done from the beginning
Expected time and place unimpeded
Given circumstances of a promise
Stone letter signed insurmountable
Sign it, seal it and hand out receipts
Round table poised and accountable
I will never make anyone a promise
That I don't intend to honor and keep
If I tell you I will always catch you
All you need do is to take the leap
A promise made is a promise kept
Swim all water to the highest peak
Found at the top of Mount Everest
Frostbite feet have seen every creek

AMY'S GARDEN

Mother and daughter send their angelic spirits
Seen in the flowers and every vacant cocoon
Four fields reverberate stories of a loss
One father said goodbye way too soon
Two angels continue to watch over visitors
A light breeze carrying upbeat emotions
Songs of the fields in the form of laughter
A father's love swimming all five oceans
A father prayed for a sign from his daughter
A widower prayed for a sign from his wife
A promise to see them again in the future
A promise he will keep in the afterlife
A butterfly wife and a sunflower daughter
Final seeds sewn around a solitary tree
A father welcomes strangers for pictures
A sixth sense allows believers to see
Janie is a mother called home too early
Amy filled our hearts for fourteen years
Each butterfly that lands on each flower
Unites all three and erases all tears
A promise made to keep two names alive
Zero doubt of two believers coming down
Seeds sewn further ignites a legacy
Mother and daughter spirits in Summertown
A single red sunflower with fourteen blooms
Loving community and a heavenly pardon
Answered prayers from a wife and a daughter
Ever present in the field of Amy's Garden
Spiritual desires accompany open invitation
And you too will also have the honor
You now know the sunflower field story
Of Amy and Janie and Tony Brawner

SHE StOPPED BY

The day was the fifteenth of November
I will write this down for my own reasons
Moonlight in her eyes on my carport
Sunlight in my eyes from all four seasons
I sang to her, "Cold" by Chris Stapleton
I got a laugh and a short salsa dance
Something stopped time for a moment
Was it her or was it I in a trance?
I offered a drink from the kitchen
She accepted and followed me inside
A decade and a half have passed by
Last time my heart beat before it died
It has risen like a phoenix from the ashes
Sending blood coursing through my veins
She said, "he isn't a good guy, is he?"
Life vaults me across the fast lanes
I say, "that's for you to decide sweetheart"
Car salesman comes over every day
My heart proceeds with cautious hesitancy
Follow the heart that won't lead astray
I rambled about books and her religion
I showed her my new laptop, I think
I sent her a poem that I have written
I also forgot to give her that drink
This heavenly creature asking questions
Feelings felt I will try to conceal
I can only hope that I caught her eye
She stopped by to say hello and chill

I MaDE A MIStaKE

I made a mistake tonight via timing
The mistakes in my life are piling up
They say, you win some and lose others
Life will not allow a contract or a prenup
I apologized for the inconvenient action
Yet the feeling of failure remains steady
Is forgiveness a necessary expectation?
That will happen if and when they're ready
How many times is too many I'm sorry's?
How often is too much to apologize?
Why sacrifice time and energy worrying?
Unable to look the person in the eyes
It is by nature that some of us care
Make no mistake, I no longer lose sleep
Our mistakes will always be relative
I ain't part of the herd of Little Bo Peep
I appreciate those who live the struggle
If you're reading, you're obviously alive
"Make no mistake" is an impossibility
Apologize. Move on. Always survive.
Do your part and admit to wrongdoing
It is the least that we can do when wrong
But remember that I tried reconciling
When my words end up heard in a song

A SaLUtE tO RInGGOLD

We honor those who fought for country
Each name on each cross describes elites
Hundreds of crosses to pay tribute
United States flags adorn our streets
Ringgold citizens sign up to assist
Within minutes all flags begin flying
Patriotic fuel for the soul increases
Thirteen stripes and fifty stars undying
Our small town in northwest Georgia
Enlisted thousands throughout the years
Fighting for freedom and principle
Depot town with many volunteers
Those Killed in Action are never lost
Forever found on the courthouse lawn
They paid for freedom with their lives
An infinity flame ensures they live on
A drive through town or sidewalk stroll
Eager search that will end with a picture
Visitors leave flowers to honor family
Others leave words from the Scripture
Memorial Day followed by Fourth of July
From the Sheriff's office to City Hall
Six weeks each year we fly Old Glory
Veterans Day is no exception in the fall
We document each loved one's location
The Annex is a good place to start
As a veteran of the United States Navy
I thank you from the bottom of my heart

Unnoticed Poet

When I begin contradictory dialog
Weakness and influence are in the directive
Combating yin and yang with acceptance
Inner warzone of the schizoaffective
Love and money cannot be avoided
Pain and tragedy will always have a seat
Train the brain to absorb exact opposites
"Go for it" in the same breath as "dead meat"
A jack of all trades plus an intellect
Humble servant called to do the right thing
Honorable and courageous protector
Forever loyal without wearing a ring
Engineering mind combined with artistry
Wear the uniform and master every sport
Fight for freedom with guns and intelligence
A finished book and a publication cohort
Constant battle with good and with evil
Place your bets and then roll the dice
Prideful hindrance of anything negative
Inspiration offered up for sacrifice
I was told I would always be subordinate
So, I created my own philosophy
It took thirteen years from start to finish
Hanging on the wall is my college degree
Potential energy can become kinetic
I love unconditionally all of my days
I wait for the right woman to love me
I can't wait to meet the children we'll raise
Financial stability alongside contentment
You'll never fall with me by your side
I'm the reason that you always feel safe
Forever present in the happy tears cried

Mental standards equaled and surpassed
Written language goes in for the kill
I call myself mentally capable
Civilization calls me mentally ill

Intention

Some sessions begin by simply writing
The destination has yet to be decided
Guided hand leaves behind uncertainty
When the pen and brain have collided
Left behind are those without belief
Pay attention to the one they call "Poet"
He can bring forth the emotion desired
You will shed that tear and you know it
Anger brought about by any given word
Fear has been felt at least once or twice
A bit of laughter thrown in for good measure
Purposely creating wisdom and sacrifice
Words can help anyone move mountains
Words bury that same soul in one sentence
Words can create an instant courage
Words have led lost souls to repentance
Words have guided generations to hate
Words are spoken to hurt with intent
Words are used to bring forth memories
Words create books after years spent
Say hello to a stranger; make sure to smile
True friendship is never allowed to die
Be there for family, friends and neighbors
Steady shoulder to hold the tears they cry
Be the reason they show up for work
Be the reason someone learns to trust
Be the wisdom sought during any crisis
Great words and good intentions are a must
So, choose every word very wisely
When it's over, how will your story look?
Like it or not, you are leaving your mark
You are constantly writing your own book

LIFtOFF

Write and smoke all day
Chosen price that I pay
I'm gettin' high to get by
Prodigal words to say
Fire up and pass the hawg
Windows up for a better fog
Release that beastly savage
Create a future dialog
We're gonna twist and burn
We're gonna twist and burn
Sit and chill for a little while
Burn when it gets your turn
With the leaves we allocate
Grab a pen and corroborate
Socialize with all cultures
Creation don't discriminate
Find the beat to tag along
Toxicology report is wrong
Liquor speaks of disaster
Funny stuff sings the song
We're gonna twist and burn
We're gonna twist and burn
Sit and chill for a little while
Burn when it gets your turn

FaLLEn NEEDLES

We go as a family on Thanksgiving
To a Christmas tree farm outside of town
Yearly arguments ensue about axe safety
We agree on the perfect tree to cut down
Then tie it to the car or toss it in the truck
Travel home to fresh turkey and dressing
We fill our plates with more than we need
Gather 'round the table to say the blessing
When bellies are full and all are finished
We tell the story of how Mary gave birth
Excitement and wonder fill up the room
Faith and grace in pictures we unearth
We align the tree with the window frame
Go to the attic and fetch decorations
Family traditions bring us all back together
Matriarch and patriarch salutations
Each year we gift each other ornaments
Each represents a memory we created
We tell stories of our ornament history
Although some may be dull and faded
Our tree will stay there for nearly a month
Shining bright and surrounded by presents
Laughs will be shared throughout the season
New memories bring back our adolescence
Plenty of pictures taken and videos recorded
We listen to The Fab Four by the Beatles
Create memories around the Christmas tree
Until time to stop sweeping up fallen needles

Most Celebrated Birthday

Documentation of holiday magic
Around the fire in your Christmas flannel
Sleigh bells ring on every child's rooftop
Christmas tunes on each radio channel
Half of each paycheck pays for presents
Peppermint spice at the coffee shop
Rudolph trains misfits for the big night
Frosty waves again at the traffic cop
Donate to the Salvation Army bucket
In Santa hats with a smile and a bell
Never been happier spending money
Prices drop and everything is on sale
Tis the season for yuletide carol folly
Snowball fights and hunting for deer
Honey ham at the center of the table
Time for Scrooge and pass Eddie a beer
Dirty Santa steals from the grownups
Family pictures by the Christmas tree
Every dollar spent will be worth it
Trust in love, magic and serendipity
Re-gifting is noticed but welcomed
They wanted that gift back anyway
Merry Christmas to all and remember
Spread cheer and have a happy holiday

Waiting for her to mend or return to sender

In a world where timing is everything, he lacked the courage to stand up and speak his mind. He sat and he waited and he died, old and lonely.

SOMETHING NEW

Progression takes a strong leap forward
Old technology is left in the dust
A loving soul has changed my circumstance
I promise to write like we discussed
A new beginning for a new future
I shall start with my visit to your house
The hospitality shown is unmatched
I admire the generosity of your spouse
We spoke about trials and tribulations
At times we both struggle to bear the cost
Amongst it all we managed to laugh
We shed tears over loved ones lost
You introduced me to many neighbors
In the loop with everyone's profession
Common courtesy must be contagious
I only hope I left a good impression
You invited me to your dinner table
Conversation as we enjoyed our meal
Each time that I type on this laptop
I'm reminded of how you made me feel
I will never forget what you have done
You embody the definition of virtue
To the land of politicians, we go
With all that I am I love and thank you

Chapter Ten

In conclusion, wait until the ride comes to a complete stop or exit at terminal velocity. Parachutes are not included. Too many times I have called upon God only to have what I called for appear. Mistakes had to be made in order to grow. My heart had to be shattered in order to become truly capable of love. Life had to be experienced in order to discover a purpose. Tomorrow's today cannot ever be yesterday; or, is it already? I hope you have enjoyed your experience within the undulant mind of my alter ego, Street Christian Devil. Thank you to all and to all a good night.

Words

Brilliant brilliance is genius
Brilliant genius is what?
Viewers will make the decision
Words just don't make the cut
So, provide us with a word
Results in thirty minutes
Can a word be verbally assaulted?
Or buried with one simple sentence?
Line up to place your bets
Found at the high stakes table
You know what is said of jealousy
It's as old as Cain and Abel
Proceed to victory lane
Cash black and white checkered chips
Pay for books and pay for tuition
Bypass the lack of scholarships
Concrete and rebar hold secrets
Lifeless words with concrete-filled lungs
Mafia word hit man legends
Words lost forever speaking in tongues
Words suppressed by gargling blood
Gasping for air in hell's handbasket
Secrets that are taken to the grave
Unspoken last words sealed in a casket

Twenty Year Mile

I won't speak of my childhood errors
In this story, I will take you back twenty
When the events play out on paper
You'll discover that twenty is plenty
It was the turn of the millennium
I was fresh out of the military
How could I know more pain lie ahead?
Future map to a false visionary
I never found my heart in the carpet mill
My new adventure as a truck vendor
Re-entry into my life in Atlanta
This will now become a mindbender
I'm unable to list all specifics
Many angels have climbed on my shoulders
A guide through impossibility
Strength to literally move boulders
She gave me the confidence I needed
To face what the future would bring
Total disregard of self to protect
Stories that tug at every heartstring
Tragic stories of pure God-fearing helplessness
Survival content is through the roof
The love story within is for the big screen
I'm left wishing I could provide more proof
Each time you complain about reality
At least you will know it is indeed real
Live your life in rapid eye movement
That's the closest to how I've felt and feel
Constant comparison to her perfection
Inner perfection lives within each soul
Memory serves and leaves but two choices
Love and be loved or six feet in a hole

I will seek the perfection within you
Providing proof that I will always care
I will open each door and answer each call
Earn the right to say I'll always be there

HERE to Stay

Another trip to hell
Another sleepless night
Another memory surfaces
Onset of another fight
Reach against the pull
Fight through the pain
Uneducated censors
Great is the black Dane
Promise of avoidance
Loyalty in every bone
Reclusive nature chosen
Heart location unknown
Repetitive twelve steps
Eternal circle day by day
Gatekeeper of the heart
To whom it was given away

Midnight Conversation

I feel called to assist in faith
Help me find a vision to portray
The words in red paint a picture
I trust that He knows what to say
I ask that I be led to witness
Use me as you will if you may
Mind travels to the River Jordan
Give me the words to convey
Soak up my inner existence
Load the wisdom and fire away
Fight the darkness that's inside
Use my fingers and I shall obey
The devil is trying to enter
The war within is underway
I ask that you stand in my corner
Your mercy I cannot repay
Social platform to reach the lost
One chance to show them the way
I asked for you to guide me
You made the choice to stay
I only hope to reach one
In Jesus Christ name I pray

So Long Yesterday

You showed me troubles and triumphs
Victories alongside disappointments
Bring forth more success and failure
Trials. Tribulations. Anointments.
Inspiration has left the premises
Signs all around point to evil
Rise up and recognize progress
Work hard for tomorrow's retrieval
Hello to the sunrise
So long mistakes I've made
Bring on tomorrow
So long yesterday
A new prospect has taken up interest
She inspires my dreams to keep burning
She introduced herself as my soulmate
Family and friends of the jury adjourning
Twenty-years spent mastering all trades
A dream to have others hear my voice
A pandemic provides other options
Words in this song reveal my choice
Hello to the sunrise
So long mistakes I've made
Bring on tomorrow
So long yesterday
I wrote a book and married my soulmate
I have lived and I can't give any more
I have said my goodbyes to family
Standing at the gates of a pearly door
Hello tomorrow
So long mistakes I've made
Hello to Heaven
So long yesterday

Мама

You busted your tail for forty plus years, Mama
Guided us through the pain and the tears, Mama
You work every night and all day, Mama
For what you've done I cannot repay, Mama
You kept us all clothed, bathed and fed, Mama
The darkest corners are where I'd tread, Mama
Saw me go through my worst times, Mama
Making choices of the worst kind, Mama
All the times that I went to jail, Mama
I'm sorry for dragging you through the hell, Mama
I'm glad I didn't see the penitentiary, Mama
That's not the man you raised me to be, Mama
Stood by me through thick and thin, Mama
It's clear you're with me until the end, Mama
Wish I could take back my mistakes, Mama
It hurts to know I made your heart ache, Mama
Know my heart is now in the right place, Mama
Can't promise but try not to disgrace, Mama
Made the man that people see today, Mama
Fought for freedom and I was betrayed, Mama
Never left me when it killed me inside, Mama
Know the flag still fills me with pride, Mama
Taught me righteousness, not of greed, Mama
I'll fight for happiness as I proceed, Mama
You taught me praise will come in due time, Mama
My love will be revealed in this rhyme, Mama
I make mistakes but love triumphs all, Mama
You continue to teach, that's why I call, Mama
I vow to fight fear and discrimination, Mama
I won't run away in any situation, Mama
Never left me and I'll never leave you, Mama

I'll use the lessons to stop the abuse, Mama
In time, the more I want it to show, Mama
My love for you won't dwindle but grow, Mama
Most will never know what I have done, Mama
Greatest gift ever was becoming your son, Mama
My only goal is always making you proud, Mama
I appreciate you and I'll say it aloud, Mama
My dearest mother, I will always appreciate you
My dearest mother, I will always appreciate you

TRULY FOREVER

Growing tired of reading the words
The audience suggestions dissipated
The words and hours spent in research
Effective prior to words left infiltrated
To never give up has left the building
Over my dead body is called by death
Retire the neurological output freedom
Breathe no more spoken last breath
Callused fingers and a deep-fried brain
The end reaching and grasping last sins
Compromise has left but one option
The end is where the next book begins
Now there aren't any pages left to turn
Success or failure relies upon fate
This chapter is over with zero regret
There is no longer a need to concentrate
Beautifully sacred sincerest of thanks
Last three lines of one subconscious
It wouldn't have happened without you
I made it to the Library of Congress

Arial and AR Darling on 50# LSI archival crème white
Type and Design by Karen Paul Stone

WHat OtHERS aRE SaYinG

"I know I'm biased, but you're absolutely one of the most brilliant writers that I have ever personally known." ~ *Nathan L.*

"What a special emotional expression of feelings in this poem! I've got cry in my throat." ~ *Janelle C.*

"You've got some mad skills." ~ *Angela M.*

ABOUt tHE AUtHOR

Born at Saint Joseph's Hospital in Stockton, California in 1977, Trenton Scott was gifted with a fascination for creativity, sports, and critical thinking. He was always drawn to competition within the sports industry, both as an athlete growing up, and as a lifelong fan. In 1995, his sports career ended on the baseball diamond in the spring, and he graduated from Ringgold High School, in Ringgold, Georgia.

In 1996, poor choices led him to join the Navy in order to better his life, and escape the environment associated with those poor choices. He ventured to make better decisions. In the Navy, he was fortunate enough to receive the Retired Officers Association Leadership Award.

After the Navy, he bounced from job to job, and thirteen years after taking his first college course, he graduated with a degree in Psychology from Dalton State College, in Dalton, Georgia, in 2008. While working for a Coca-Cola Bottling Company in Cleveland, Tennessee, his Schizoaffective Disorder worsened, and he started writing again.

CPSIA information can be obtained
at www.ICGtesting.com
Printed in the USA
LVHW091358190221
679376LV00005B/41

9 781947 589391